Praise fo

"A year or so after we featured Isaiah
117 on an episode of Returning the
Favor, I saw that Ronda Paulson had
publicly thanked 'Jesus Christ and Mike
Rowe' for the sudden expansion of her
remarkable foundation. Obviously, I was
flattered, though under no delusion that
the former had been more instrumental
than the latter. But it should also be
noted that somewhere in between me
and the Son of God, are many thousands of good people who have been
sincerely touched by Ronda's efforts to
fix our broken foster care system. When
those people saw what Ronda was doing,
and the impact she was having on so
many kids in terrible circumstances, they
stepped up to support her organization.
Being good people, they simply had no
choice. Fair warning—when you finish
this book, you won't, either."

—Mike Rowe, Television Host

HE'S INVITING US IN

The Story of Isaiah 117 House

RONDA PAULSON

STREAMLINE
BOOKS

HE'S INVITING US IN

The Story of Isaiah 117 House

Cover Design by Streamline Books

Streamline Books

www.WriteMyBooks.com

Paperback ISBN: 9-798-3924-1353-9

Hardcover ISBN: 9-798-3924-1373-7

July 18th, 2023

Dedication

To the fair-skinned, red-headed, chubby nine-month-old I met on November 5, 2015—you forever changed me, my heart, and my whole understanding of what it means to be a mom. You have turned me into a fierce advocate for those without a voice, and for that I am forever grateful.

To the littlest member of the Paulson family—March 30, 2017, completed our family with a gift we never knew we needed. Your joy and your dimples have melted all of us. Your story of resilience led to the formation of Eli's Law, which continues to protect those who cannot protect themselves.

Isaiah and Eli, you opened our eyes to a world we never knew existed. I am so grateful I get to be your mom.

And to Corey, Sophie, and Mac—I would not want to ride this crazy train with anyone else. Corey, your willingness to step into the crazy. Sophie, your love for all children. Mac, your constant calm in the storm. Together, your collective willingness to open your hearts, love unconditionally, support in ways others may never see, and pick up the slack when mom is on the road do not go unnoticed.

Paulson Party of Six—I love you more than chocolate!

Contents

Foreword

by Jonathan "JP" Pokluda

Throughout the 16 years that I've been a pastor, I've learned that ministry luncheons are just a reality of church work. There are many kinds of organizations that advocate for different groups of people. There are ministries that seek to help the homeless, orphans, babies in the womb, and so many other great and biblical causes. You've probably been to one of these kinds of luncheons before. Most often you get a portion of overcooked chicken, a side of vegetables, hear from an activist about a cause they're passionate about, and then be propositioned with an ask to give towards said cause. I've been there many times.

So when I went to the Isaiah 117 House luncheon, I thought I knew what to expect. It was at a venue on the outskirts of Waco, where these sorts of things are often hosted. I checked in and saw many of the familiar faces. Surprisingly the chicken wasn't overcooked, but the menu was predictable. I sat at a table with several others from our church and the event progressed as I expected with someone doing an introduction of the speaker.

Then, a cheerful, middle-aged woman with a thick Southern accent came to the platform with a microphone. I learned her name was Ronda Paulson and she was the founder of the organization. I expected her to be articulate and inspiring. But what happened next, I couldn't have expected. I leaned in, I laughed hard, and I was left in tears. It wasn't simply that the talk was well-delivered. It was (and this might be foreign to some of you) that The Holy Spirit moved in that room. It was that the message she shared was hard-fought for. She wasn't just advocating for children in the foster system. She was vulnerably sharing her own journey in a way that was so honest, relatable, and entertaining.

It was obvious to me that God called her to this mission. Her goals were so big that only God would be a suitable partner to them. Her fight was fierce. Her approach was strategic. She clearly addressed the many problems I had witnessed firsthand in our foster system. She didn't just point out the gaps—she stood in them. And when she was done sharing, I wanted to stand in them with her. In hindsight, there was real risk to attending the luncheon that day. As I got in my car to leave, I was a different person than the one who had pulled up an hour and a half earlier. God had done a work in my heart.

Our church became a financial partner to the Isaiah 117 house in Waco. I am so thankful for God's work through Ronda. The story she shared that day is the same story on the pages ahead. It will be in greater detail and even more inspiring than when I heard it. That means there's a risk to you, the reader. When you turn the final page of the last chapter, you will be a different person than the one who is about to turn the page now. Make sure you're up for that and enjoy the journey!

Introduction

I often tell people I can't wait to get to heaven and ask God why He chose to use us. Because, when I think about God and His infinite wisdom, grace, kindness, and power, and then I think about us—flawed, sinful, broken people— it's shocking to me that He would want to use us. And yet as I study Scripture and examine my own life, one thing is clear: God always has and continues still to invite us into His work. He wants to use us.

As I've walked with God, I have slowly learned how to recognize His invitations, and, maybe more importantly, how to say yes to them. This crazy journey I've been on throughout, well, my whole life, but especially with Isaiah 117 House, has taught me that He not only invites us in, but He also turns our yeses—including the scared and unsure ones—into amazing things we never could have imagined.

God's invitations, even when they're to something way outside of our abilities and comfort zones, lead to blessings for us and for others. And, when we hand Him our scared, unsure yes, He fully equips us for whatever He's called us to do as we work together to further His kingdom.

In 2017, I handed God a scared, little yes, and I've watched Him take off ever since. Houses have been built. Children have been loved. Families have been supported. Resources have been provided.

This is the beauty of the God we serve.

Let me be perfectly clear—there is absolutely nothing special about me to cause God to use me, to cause God to bring any good from my one very small, very imperfect life. My story is yours.

Or, it could be yours.

Why? Because God is present and active and close with all of His people, and He speaks to us more often than we realize. He's working, and He's inviting us in.

Isaiah 1:19 says that if you are willing and obedient, you will taste the best of the land. Working in foster care and child welfare is hard and it's heavy. But working alongside God is the best of the land.

As you read this book, I hope you don't just hear the story of Isaiah 117 House. I hope you don't for one second think, *Wow, look at what Ronda has done.* I hope you hear the overwhelming call of the Father, who is inviting you, too, into His work on this earth so that He may be glorified. He's inviting us in. All of us. Let's say yes together.

Chapter One

We got "the call" at about 3:30 on a fall afternoon in 2015. I and my two kids, Sophie and Mac, ages twelve and nine, were gathered around the kitchen island after school, eating a snack and getting started on homework. Then my phone rang.

The caseworker on the other end of the line introduced herself and said, "I'm calling on behalf of the Carter County, Tennessee, Department of Children's Services, and we have a nine-month-old little boy who needs a home." As she gave a few more details, I remember thinking, *This is it. This is the day we say yes.*

Now, as you may learn about me throughout this book, I'm not normally one to ask permission for anything from anybody besides the Lord. But this was definitely not a normal situation. I took a deep breath and responded, "Ma'am, I'm going to do something very uncharacteristic."

"What's that?"

I laughed and said, "I'm going to ask my husband if this is okay." I told her I'd call her back and then gave my husband, Corey, a call at work as Sophie pestered me with questions and Mac stared at the counter. When he answered, I started this life-defining conversation with a sentence that I'm sure every husband longs to hear at some point in their marriage:

"Corey, tell me you'll love me no matter what."

He thought that was my way of telling him I'd wrecked the car again, but I told him that wasn't it and then repeated myself. "Tell me you'll love me no matter what."

Here's the thing: Corey was cautious about the idea of becoming a foster family. He had graciously gone through the training with me to become a foster parent (more on that later) and had always encouraged me to obey promptings from the Holy Spirit, but taking in a baby was a whole new thing. Taking in a baby was a step of obedience that would launch our entire family into a new way of life. Once we said yes, our family could never go back to the way we had been before.

So I kept talking. I wanted to make sure that if Corey said yes, it would be his truest answer, since if he said yes it would be our final answer.

"We can't say yes to this unless *we* say yes to this," I said. "There can be no future day down the road when it's hard and messy and we're tired, and you turn to me and say 'You wanted this.' That can't ever happen. We're either fully in this together, or we're not. I gotta know."

By this time he knew what I was getting at. "There's a baby."

"There's a baby," I responded.

Immediately, he said, "I'm on my way."

Even though he only worked about three minutes from our house, we were all a hot mess by the time he arrived. And if you didn't already know, let me tell you: mommas feel the stress of everybody. Corey was tense. Sophie was over-the-moon excited. And Mac, unfortunately, was silent.

Corey and Sophie walked out the back door to our minivan first, and as Mac and I followed he turned to me and asked, "Is it a boy or a girl?"

"It's a boy."

"Then I don't want it."

When I tell you that the mom guilt hit me *so hard* in that moment, I mean it hit me like a punch in the stomach. Instantly, the uncertainties began to flood in. *What am I doing to my biological children in saying yes to this? Is this really the right thing for our family to be doing? How do I say yes to the call that I've received from God and also care for my family in the best way possible?* I encouraged him as best I could, but my words seemed to fall flat. He walked out with his shoulders slumped to get in the minivan.

Now, I don't know how God communicates with you personally, or what you even believe about Him, but I know He knows how much I value comedic relief, because sometimes He talks to me in pretty funny ways. This was one of those times. As I went to get in the van, I noticed a flier that had been placed under the windshield wipers, as if we were parked somewhere like the Walmart. Except we weren't at the Walmart, we were in our driveway at home. So, I wondered, why was there a flier on my car? I grabbed the piece of paper as I got in and then yelled out to my family, "Guys, we've got this!" They looked at me, all feeling their varying emotions about what was going down, and I said, "This is a message from the Lord. We've got this."

I held up the paper for them so they could see what I saw: a plain white piece of paper with nothing else on it besides, of all things, a little cartoon penguin. At the top it said, "You can do it!" and across the bottom: "Motivational penguin." It still hangs on our fridge today.

So, yep, I believe that God is funny. No one can tell me that that piece of paper was not from Him. Why else in the world would it be there at the exact moment we needed encouragement? It's in tiny moments like that when I'm reminded that God is sovereign. In fact, I am met with His unlimited, creative, and, yes, sometimes funny provision every single time I step out in obedience. Sometimes His provision looks like a huge donation for your nonprofit;

sometimes it looks like a motivational penguin stuck on your windshield. I'll take 'em both.

Unfortunately, Mr. Motivational Penguin could only do so much to ease the stress we were all feeling as we made the quick drive to the case-worker's office. We were instructed to go to the back door, and when we parked, Mac refused to get out. The fact that Mac was the most easygoing, obedient kid I'd ever met made his resistance hit that much harder. Eventually, Corey, Sophie, and I got out, and the caseworker opened her door.

I'll never forget the moment I first saw Isaiah. He was a fair-skinned, chubby nine-month-old with big blue eyes and a full head of fiery red hair, balancing on the caseworker's hip. His outfit was way too small for him, and that was what I asked the caseworker about first.

"We know it's too small," she responded. "But the outfit he was in when he came to us was so filthy that we had to get rid of it, and this is all we could find in our office."

She went on to say that they had tried to clean him up before our arrival, but that the best they could do was give him a sponge bath in the sink they used for drug testing. As we kept talking, we all remained standing partially outside, looking into the doorway. A nervous family facing a tired caseworker holding a dirty, innocent baby. It was a heartbreaking, awkward moment, but looking back I see that all along a thread of redemption ran bright and strong through that scene.

Then, she handed him to us.

Someone else passed us his diaper bag but told us not to bring it into our house for twelve to twenty-four hours so that the roaches would have time to crawl out. All this time, this sweet baby was in my arms, smiling from ear to ear, smelling like he hadn't had a bath in days. My heart could have exploded over the unfairness he had already experienced in his little life.

I quickly realized that in all of our preparation (all ten minutes of it), we hadn't thought to bring a car seat. Keep in mind, the Paulson family had not had a baby in the home for nine years. And we had been operating from the assumption that no more babies were coming, so we had gotten rid of everything. The caseworker brought out the only option they had: a dirty, old car seat, which we loaded him into.

As we got ready to drive away, I finally asked the caseworker his name.

"Isaiah."

Isaiah. We didn't know it at the time, but we had just met the newest member of the Paulson family.

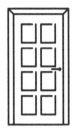

A Note from the House

OUR VERY FIRST *guest at the Isaiah 117 House was not who I expected, although I'm not sure that I could have told you what my expectations actually were. Looking back now, I can't imagine our first guest being anyone other than who it was! Julia was a six-year-old with beautiful, long, blond hair who loved all things sparkly and sweet. At such a young age, she had already seen more sadness and uncertainty than any child should.*

She came to us from an organization called Safe Families, which works with biological parents to try and prevent the child from being removed permanently from their home. Safe Families provides a home willing to take the child in temporarily in the hope that the child will return to their own bed in a matter of weeks.

Through Safe Families, Julia had been living with a wonderful lady, Anna, for a few weeks. They had done all the things—made cupcakes, bought new clothes, played with bubbles and toys as often as she'd wanted— and Julia had felt safe. Unfortunately, however, the mom failed to meet the standards required by the state to receive her daughter back into her care. So, a few days later, a caseworker found herself sitting at a McDonald's with this sweet little girl and this sweet lady, telling them that Julia had to leave Anna and come into the state's custody.

Julia's eyes filled with tears, and she wrapped herself around Anna's arm. "I don't want to leave Ms. Anna. She takes my fears away."

At that, Anna started to cry, and the caseworker sat there, a lump growing in her own throat as she thought of having to take this child away from her primary source of comfort in such an uncertain time. But then it hit her: she didn't have to take her to the office! Julia didn't have to go sit in a cubicle or conference room anymore.

The caseworker leaned across the table and said, "Hey, would you like to come with me to the Isaiah 117 House?" Julia looked up through her tears, and she went on. "It's the most fun house. We can play outside! We can paint your nails if you want to. We can have a snack. Why don't you just come check it out with me?"

We had opened our doors for the first time ever at 8:00 that morning. By noon, we got the call that Julia was on her way. And I got to greet her at the door.

We were still finishing up the final touches around the house, and Julia immediately wanted to help. In no time, she had set her bag of belongings in the living room, picked out a pair of new shoes from our donated selection —a pair of obnoxious and adorable light-up, little-girl heels—and was clomping along right next to me all over that house.

She got to choose a new stuffed animal, too, and a decent portion of our afternoon went to sending that stuffed animal down the slide in the backyard about 400 times. She'd kept a picture of her and Ms. Anna in her duffle bag. Every now and then she paused, looked up at me, and said, "Can I show you my picture of Ms. Anna?"

We always stopped, and she would let me hold the picture as she told me about the fun they'd had. Thinking back to her time with Ms. Anna often made her cry, and we sat and mourned that separation together as she processed her losses, changes, and uncertainties.

Eventually I would get us moving again, making cookies, going back outside, or playing dress-up. But Julia received as much attention and space as she wanted to talk about Ms. Anna, about the family she was leaving, and about what was ahead.

She was only with us for about six hours. A foster family was found, and she left to go to that new placement. But I locked the doors of the Isaiah 117 House at the end of that first day forever changed.

I prayed that those six hours had meant as much to her as they had meant to me. I prayed for her continued safety and that she would adjust well to the foster home. I prayed that she left the house feeling more seen and at peace than when she entered. Mostly, I prayed that somewhere deep in her heart, she believed more firmly that she was not alone and that she was loved and worthy of love.

That doesn't just happen in a loud office with phones ringing, copiers beeping, and people going about their days meeting deadlines and making plans for lunch. That happens in a home with a volunteer who is there to focus solely on the well-being of that child.

Our first guest was not who I thought it would be, but she was perfect. The house did what the house was created to do. That day, Isaiah 117 House reduced trauma for a child.

Chapter Two

I look back on the day we met Isaiah and honestly can't believe we said yes. In hindsight, it made no sense. It had been nine years and a vasectomy since we'd had a baby in our home, and we had sold or given away all the baby-related things. Yet, on that day in 2015, we said yes to a nine-month-old.

And God made it so clear to us that even though we felt (and honestly were) so unequipped to take in a baby, He was going to provide every step of the way. Some of the most obvious and practical provisions came from the community of people who came around us to help. I still can't get over it.

One friend, in particular, was so ready to help that she actually beat us home. When we pulled up to our house, there stood Amy Jensen, literally holding a pink baby bathtub, Johnson & Johnson baby wash, and a new outfit for a boy. I hadn't had time to tell anyone how much this baby in our backseat needed a bath, but God knew, and He sent Amy to our house with everything we needed. When she tried to apologize for the bathtub being pink, I wouldn't let her because I was simply so grateful to her and to the Lord.

We immediately gave him a bath—which he loved—and then put him in the one outfit that he now owned. It was already almost too small for him, but it worked for that day.

After his bath, I dug in the diaper bag and found one bottle (which I scrubbed and scrubbed and *scrubbed*) and just enough baby formula to last him the day. And with those things—a bath, an outfit, and dinner—we began to care for this baby we had just met.

We had to be gone from our house for about an hour that evening, and by the time we got back, more friends had shown up at our house. This time, however, they didn't just wait on our front porch. They had found a way inside and were in the guest room of our house, setting up a crib and baby monitor. I hadn't even thought about getting a baby monitor, but again, God knew.

After everything was set up, we all sat in our living room, and one of the little boys, Caleb, walked across the room to me and asked, "Where's his shoes?" I told him that Isaiah didn't have any shoes, and Caleb started crying. He turned to his mom and said through his tears, "Momma, did you hear that? He doesn't have any shoes. We have to get him shoes."

My heart melted at how tender his heart was towards Isaiah. This little boy saw someone innocent and defenseless in need, and he knew they had to do something to help. And, as it turned out, Caleb's reaction was a response that we saw from people of all ages over the coming days. I hold to a sincere belief that when it comes to needs that exist in places like foster care, it's not that God's people don't care—they just don't know. But boy, when God's people *do* know, when they *do* see needs that they're able to meet, they *act*.

Our doorbell started ringing, and it didn't stop. Over the next few days, people brought us clothes, blankets, diapers, and wipes. They brought us baby food, formula, a high chair, and meals. One couple even knocked on our door with $500 for us to spend on whatever we needed. People just kept showing up. And I'm not just talking close personal friends. People we didn't really even know also gave generously to us. It was incredible. Over and over, kind people kept telling me different versions of the same thing: "I heard about what you're doing, and I want to help."

I understood the importance of community in a new light during those first days with Isaiah. If we hadn't had the support that we did, I don't know how we would've done it. How does anyone say yes to something like that without having others to come around them?

The heartbreak of a broken family was met by the beauty of community in a new way for me through this first foster-care experience. It made my heart swell with the feeling that something more could and should be done to help those in the world of foster care.

EVEN WITH A STRONG COMMUNITY, there is quite the learning curve to navigate when you're a new foster parent. Especially when you're a new foster parent who is also remembering how to care for an infant. I remember we had what felt like an endless stream of meetings and appointments with Isaiah, which at times felt overwhelming to keep up with.

One day Isaiah had an appointment with the pediatrician, and in order to get him there on time I had to leave work early. I was so tired and frazzled and just plain worn out from the nonstop schedule. After running to pick up Isaiah, I then had to drive back across town to the doctor's office, and to add to the stress, from the moment I strapped him in his car seat Isaiah was absolutely bawling his eyes out.

Of course, I'd had two babies before so I knew: babies do that. But still, I was already upset, and then he was upset, and both of us being upset was more than I could take. I didn't have anything to calm him down, but what I did have was a bottle of Ibuprofen *with a tightly closed lid* that sounded a lot like a rattle. And I was desperate.

Now, this may be one of those stories that you're supposed to leave out of a book, but it's an important one. Besides, after nine years, I can still attest that everyone is okay, so here we go.

I shook the bottle a little bit, which seemed to calm him down, so I let him hold it. For a minute it seemed like Operation Save Our Sanity was working, but then in the rearview mirror I watched as he shook the bottle and the lid flew off, showering pills everywhere.

I scrambled to pull over to the side of the road as fast as I could. At this point, I'm not sure if I was actually yelling or if I was too busy screaming in my head for sound to escape my mouth, but I know I was terrified that this child who I'd only had for a few days was going to overdose on Ibuprofen.

The pills had fallen all across his lap. I frantically began to scoop them up and swabbed his mouth to make sure he hadn't already eaten any. My tears splashed onto his dinosaur onesie as I silently berated myself for being the absolute worst mom and wondering who in the world would give a child a bottle of pills no matter how tight the lid seemed to be. I mean, seriously, they had just given me this kid to keep him safe! What was I thinking?

As I checked for the twentieth time to make sure I'd found every pill, Isaiah sat calm for the first time that afternoon, looking up at me as if asking, "Whatcha doing?" At least one of us had calmed down.

My tears did not stop once I got back in the driver's seat. The reality of what had just happened continued to become more real to me. It could have been so bad.

Far too quickly, Isaiah began to cry again, and I officially gave up all hope of making it to that pediatric appointment.

At that moment, a Rachel Platten song came on the radio that I had never heard before.

"*. . . When you can't rise, well I'll crawl with you on hands and knees*"

"*Love, if your wings are broken, borrow mine so yours can open too . . .*"

and then the chorus:

"I'm gonna stand by you / Even if we're breaking down, we can find a way to break through / Even if we can't find heaven, I'll walk through hell with you / Love, you're not alone. I'm gonna stand by you."

A deep conviction came over me, and I sat still until the song had ended. As I gathered my wits about me I said out loud to Isaiah, my voice still wobbly, "I know we just met each other, and I know that I haven't done the best job yet, but I promise I'm not leaving you. I will walk through this with you, whatever that looks like. I am here and we will do this. I'm not going anywhere."

That song became our anthem. I don't know Rachel Platten or her intentions behind that song, but I can't hear it without thinking of foster care. So many times in foster care, there is no "heaven" on this side of heaven. There's not always a happy ending where things work out the way we think they should. Fostering is not an easy ministry; there is pain and heartache and court hearings and doctors appointments and a host of other hard things.

But those are just the challenges. True foster care—what makes it beautiful and worthwhile and deeply necessary—is the commitment. It is saying to the child you've been given to care for, "No matter how hard this is, no matter how long you're with me, I'm going to stay. I'm going to walk through this with you, and you are going to be able to count on me. No matter how this goes, I'm gonna stand by you."

That day, we found our Isaiah song.

Little did I know that a couple years later it would become our Isaiah 117 House anthem.

I HAVE a confession I need to make: It is really hard for me to focus on the beauty in a situation when I've been without sleep for several consecutive nights.

I wish I could change it, but I am probably one of the worst middle-of-the-night mommas you will ever meet. In this particular aspect of running a happy home, my kids would probably tell you that my motto is, "I don't care what's going on, just go to sleep!"

One night (or maybe I should say, very early one morning), when we were still struggling to find our new rhythm as a family, Corey and I were sitting together taking turns on baby duty. And let me tell you, it's a lot harder to focus on the miracles around you when it's 4:30 in the morning and you feel like you've thrown your back out from holding a 23-pound baby all night long. We looked at each other, and I could feel the same question hanging heavily between us. We were confident that God had led us every step of the way, but as I'm sure you can see, even though we knew it was right, it was definitely not easy. We looked at each other in the dim light, Corey holding that smiling, way-too-wide-awake little boy in his arms, and I could sense us both asking, "How did we get here?"

I'm still discovering the answer to that question. All I knew was that up to that point, my life had included some pretty unique experiences and that saying yes to God often brought me somewhere I didn't expect. And let's be real, sometimes those "somewheres" were places that I had actively fought against. But, as I keep saying yes to God, and as I keep allowing Him to direct my life, I continue to better understand how glad I am that His ways are not mine. His ways are higher and more beautiful and crazy and

story-telling-worthy than I could've ever
dreamed.

So before I go on with *this* story, I need to go
back. God had been teaching me to say yes to
crazy things for a long time.

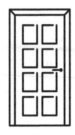

A Note from Corey

I THOUGHT FOSTERING and adopting sounded scary, emotional, and exhausting. And it has been all of those things.

But what I didn't expect it to be was so life-giving. What I didn't understand was that the love you give being a foster parent is exactly the kind of love God wants you to experience—it's unconditional, sacrificial, patient, and kind. Foster care and adoption are all of those things.

From the moment Isaiah entered our home, I was in love. In love with him, in love with the energy in our home, in love with the way our family was working together to welcome our new family member—all of it. Isaiah didn't have to do anything, and he was loved.

Yes, it interrupted our usual routine, but this new routine was better. And his presence seemed to bring an unusual peace to our home amid all the crazy. I fell in love with my wife all over again. I fell in love with my biological children even more as I watched them care for this boy that wasn't their "brother" like he was their brother. I was experiencing love like I never had before.

Foster care is scary, emotional, and exhausting. But I never expected it to bring our original family closer together. I did not expect it to change our lives the way it did. I thought we would help change a child's life, but I didn't expect the change that came to our family. I believe our family is as healthy as it is today because of our foster care journey. And that is because we were living and loving the way God intended—unconditional, sacrificial, patient, and kind.

God calls us to defend the orphan and fatherless, and I believe that's because He knows that when we do, we experience love and life the way He does. This is His plan, His nature. He invites us into His world as orphans and loves us unconditionally, sacrificially, with patience and kindness—just as we welcomed and loved our foster children.

When you choose to foster and adopt, I believe you get to experience God and love the way He intended. It can be scary, emotional, and exhausting, but it is one of the most life-giving things you can do.

I never expected that.

Chapter Three

I vividly remember the first time it hit me that God actually wants to use me in the work that He's doing. It happened one day in college.

Corey and I both attended Milligan University, located in Northeast Tennessee. It has a beautiful campus with one particularly infamous feature: Sutton Hill. It was well known that no matter how in shape you were, it was almost impossible to walk up this hill without running out of breath by the time you got to the top. Unfortunately, this fact was reestablished for us students every day; everything we needed for classes and activities was at the bottom of Sutton Hill, and everything we needed for eating and sleeping was at the top. So, yes, we spent a lot of time on this hill.

Throughout college, I felt a strong and growing desire for God to use me, but I didn't know how to make myself useful to Him. So, one day as I climbed Sutton Hill, I was praying. It was a tentative, hesitant prayer that probably went something like, "Uh, I don't feel worthy to ask this, God. I'm far from perfect, but I want to be used by You. Whatever it looks like—I want to be used by you."

One of Milligan's dorms is located right at the top of the hill, and my good friend Rob ran a ministry that was headquartered in the basement of that dorm. When I reached the end of my climb, Rob happened to be standing there outside of the building.

He waved me down and said, "Ronda, this is crazy—we were just talking about you! We want to start a new program where we focus on international medical missions, and we need a student ambassador. We think you'd be perfect for that role."

I was shocked. A prayer I had literally just asked had been answered. I hadn't realized that God worked that quickly or answered prayers like that in such a real way, but I'd said I was ready, and I was. Rob asked if I needed to think about it.

"No," I responded. "I know I'm supposed to say yes to this."

I walked away from him with my mouth hanging open, not knowing details, not knowing what the role would look like, not knowing much of anything. But I did know one thing. For the first time, I was positive that God wanted to include me in His greater work. He wasn't waiting for perfection from me; He was waiting for a prayer. All I had to do was ask.

From that moment on, I decided that I'd found my new prayer. I call it the Yes Prayer. It's the one that says, "God, I need You. I want to be used by You. I don't know what that looks like, but whatever it is, I'll say yes." It's a prayer of humility, obedience, and surrender. It acknowledges that God doesn't need me to accomplish His plans, but that I believe He *wants* me to be part of it. It acknowledges that God's ways are better than mine, and that I trust Him enough to say yes even when I don't understand.

FAST-FORWARD A FEW YEARS. Corey and I were newly married and living in an apartment in the exact dorm where that conversation with Rob had taken place. (Isn't it funny how God works?) We were "dorm parents" at that point; Corey worked in Milligan's admissions department, and I taught at a nearby high school.

I was doing a Beth Moore study on Moses and had been reading about the burning bush. If you've ever done a Beth Moore study, you know that they are seriously deep, so I was learning more about the burning bush than I'd ever known in my life.

One night I was finishing up my study in bed with Corey asleep beside me. I closed my Bible, turned off my lamp, and lay there in the dark.

"God, I don't want to need a burning bush," I remember saying. "Moses may have needed a huge burning sign in front of him in order to be convinced to obey, but I don't want to need anything like that. If You ask me to do something, I'm going to just do it. No burning bush required for me."

Now, in case you might be tempted in any way to admire me for that prayer, let me make it abundantly clear that I went to sleep that night feeling way too good about myself. It was very much a "holier than thou" feeling . . . about me versus Moses. I wish I was embellishing my own sense of arrogance in that prayer.

Well, God was ready to put my claims to the test.

The next morning I was brushing my teeth, minding my own more-faithful-than-Moses business, when I heard in my head, *Go teach step aerobics to group home girls.* I stopped mid-scrub and started laughing. I thought I must have had a crazy dream related to the girls I taught who lived in the Christian group home in our town. It was an out-of-the-blue yet very specific thought, and I moved on with my day.

I got to my classroom at the school, and fourth period—the class that those group home girls were in—rolled around. As they walked in and I said hello, I heard it again: *Go teach step aerobics to group home girls.* This time, I paused and asked myself what in the world was happening to me. I concluded that I simply needed more coffee, and I finished out the school day.

After school, I was sitting at my desk grading papers, and I heard it again, more clearly than ever: *Go teach step aerobics to group home girls.* At this point I knew it was the Lord, and I answered Him.

"Listen, this is funny and all," I said out loud to my empty classroom. "But, like, you can't just go to a group home and say, 'Hey nice to meet you; I want to teach step aerobics here please.'"

I kept talking (read: arguing) with God as I drove home. I had so many reasons to say no to such a crazy assignment!

Number one: I didn't teach step aerobics. I didn't know the first thing on how to teach something like that.

Two: Wouldn't there be a fingerprinting process or some kind of extensive background check? I couldn't just show up and start a class, right?

Three: When would I even have time to do something like that? When would the girls have time? They probably wouldn't even be open to something like that.

And then I felt, deep in my being, the words: *I thought you didn't need a burning bush.*

Well played, Lord, well played!

So then I tried another tactic with God. I decided I would obey, but only so we could both see how impossible it would be to make the idea happen. I turned my car toward the girls home, and told God the whole way there, "Watch this. We'll see who's right."

A few minutes later, I knocked on the door of the group home. A woman answered, and I jumped right in.

"Hi," I said. "My name is Ronda Paulson, and I would like to teach step aerobics to the girls here."

Without missing a beat, she responded, "Come on in! I'll call a meeting."

As you may have already noticed in these stories, one of the themes of my life is my surprise when God provides in unpredictable ways. This is another one of those times. I followed her inside as she gathered the girls in the living room and told them they had a special guest speaker.

What?

The girls sat down in front of me, and, because I couldn't think of anything else to say, I began, "I'm here because I would like to do step aerobics with you on Saturday mornings."

And then words started coming out of my mouth that I know were from the Lord.

"Listen, I know some of you," I said. "Let's just talk openly and honestly for a minute. I see you walking around the school with your head down. I know many of you are sad, and I know many of you are depressed. For me, I don't move my body to be skinny. I've given up on that, but I do move my body because it makes me feel better. And if we could do something together on Saturday mornings that makes us all feel better, I think we should do that."

They were in. I was amazed. God was providing.

I drove home, still not knowing how I was going to actually teach a step aerobics class with these girls in a few days, but now more convinced than ever that God was in this and would provide. As I walked to my apartment, I ran into a friend named Gina and ended up telling her the whole story, concluding with my current predicament. At that point, she smiled at me and said, "Did you know that I'm a certified step aerobics teacher?"

"What? Are you kidding me?"

"I'm not kidding, and I'll go with you."

Just like that, my concern about not knowing how to teach the class was taken care of. The only other things we needed were the steps and some weights. I called a lady who'd been a neighbor of mine and who had taught step aerobics.

After I explained everything to her, she let out a laugh and responded, "You know, I was just telling somebody, I have all these extra steps and weights that I am wanting to get rid of because I'm not teaching an aerobics class anymore."

I drove to her house that same day, and she filled up my Honda Civic with enough steps and weights for the whole class.

Gina and I went to that group home every Saturday morning for a long time after that. That ministry was so clearly of God, and it created, among other things, the beautiful opportunity to develop mentorship relationships. One of the girls and I spent a lot of time together, not only in step aerobics but also shopping, eating out, and talking about life. She reached back out to me years later to thank me and tell me about her own family that she was now raising with her husband.

I don't deserve credit for any good that came from the Saturday morning step aerobics in a local girls group home. All I did was say yes. God did the rest. In one day, He gave me the idea, nudged me multiple times to actually listen and act on it, and provided everything I needed. The path kept opening up before me as I kept taking steps forward.

I couldn't have told you this back in 1999 when I was in the middle of living this story. But, now that I look back, I can see that these fundamental truths of what it looks like to obey God were settling deep into my bones. You don't have to be qualified. You don't have to have all the answers. If God asks you to do something, chances are, it's going to sound totally crazy at first. But, as He kept proving to me, He will absolutely equip you for whatever's coming. Our only job is to keep saying yes.

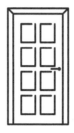

A Story from the House

WE HAD *a non-verbal little girl come to our house one afternoon, and at first we had a hard time communicating with her. Nothing we tried seemed to work. She ended up sitting at the dining room table where we had Mason jars full of crayons. She took out all the crayons and sorted them into piles based on color. If you moved one, she would just look at you and then look away and put the crayon right back. That was basically the only acknowledgment we could get that she knew we were even in the room.*

Then, a volunteer mentioned, "What about a stuffed animal?" I grabbed a big, pink, floppy-eared dog and brought it over to her.

"Hey, would you like this doggy to be yours?" She looked up and looked at the dog. Her eyes got wide and her face broke into a big smile. She took that dog and hugged and

kissed it, and then she tucked it under her chin. "What would you like to name your dog?" I asked. She just looked at me, and I said, "What if we named your dog Emily?" Emily was her caseworker's name. The little girl gave a tiny nod. "Emily it is," I said.

She carried Emily the floppy-eared dog all over the house. Emily went to the playground. Emily ate with her. Emily never left her side, and when it was time for her to go, we packed up all her new things and sent her and Emily on their way.

The next day I saw a post on Facebook from a lady I went to church with. The post was thanking Isaiah 117 House for helping to provide everything they needed while they fostered, and the picture was of the little girl laying in bed with Emily tucked under her arm. I messaged the lady and said, "Just so you know, the doggy's name is Emily."

"Oh my word," she responded. "We've just been calling it Doggy. Emily it is."

About three months later, I saw another post of this same little girl. It was a picture of her from the back looking up at something, and Emily the dog was still right there with her, being held tightly. That was when I realized the importance of a child having something that's theirs on the day of removal. They need something they can hold *onto, something they can cling to, and something they can take with them as they begin a journey they never asked for.*

We cannot change everything about removal day. We cannot take away all the pain. But we can absolutely step in with love and meet immediate needs. We can lavish love on them even through floppy-eared stuffed animals to help them know they are not alone.

Chapter Four

About five years later, Corey and I had moved and now had Sophie. We lived in a nice neighborhood, but there were some apartments at the end of our street that looked pretty rough. You just knew tough things happened there. Driving by those apartments day after day, I couldn't believe I lived so close to a place that could clearly use some hope and yet I didn't know what to do about it. So, I began praying my Yes Prayer, asking God to show me what to do—to use me in whatever way He wanted to for those people.

One day as I drove by, I heard the Lord speak to me. I felt deep in my spirit the clear words, *Take soup.*

Ummm, surely out of all the things these people might need—their electric bill paid, affordable and safe child care—*soup* was at the bottom of their list. It felt like the most ridiculous thing I'd ever heard. And, since I apparently still hadn't learned that God specializes in ideas that sound crazy, I laughed it off. But, once again, I couldn't shake the idea.

I kept making excuses about why I shouldn't do it, but God wouldn't let go. So, one night during a small group that I was hosting at my house, I decided to throw the idea out to them. I figured one of two things would happen. Option A: they'd get on board and we'd do it. Option B: they'd say it was crazy, which would make me mad, and then I'd argue both them and myself into why we needed to do it. Either way, we'd take the soup, and then I could stop feeling "*take soup*" every time I drove by. Win-win.

I got everyone's attention and told them I'd been feeling that we were supposed to take soup to the apartments down the street. They stared at me, and someone said, "Soup? Like, *soup*, soup?"

"Yep. I feel really strongly that we're supposed to take soup."

44

Immediately, the room broke into two groups. One group fixated on the logistics. If we're going to take soup, how much soup and what types of soup do we take? Should we take crackers, cornbread, muffins? Do we need tables, napkins? Who's getting these things? Are we also trying to start a Bible study? How long will it be? They were completely stuck in a tangled mess of logistics, and it was paralyzing them.

The other group was just straight-up skeptical. They didn't know why we would take soup or what our end goal would be. Both groups had honest, fair questions, and I didn't have clear answers. But, God was giving us an opportunity to serve our community in His name. It wasn't our job to have all the answers; it was our job to do the next right thing. And if all we had was the simple, open-ended directive to "take soup," then that was the main thing that mattered.

"Listen, I don't know how—we're just doing it," I finally said. "Whoever wants to be part of this, next Sunday night, we're taking soup. Okay?"

Next Sunday night, there we were: a group of people with crockpots and some crackers and napkins. (In case you were wondering, we decided on taco soup and potato soup.) We set up at some picnic tables outside the apartments and waited.

It was like a ghost town. We could see people peeking out from behind their curtains, obviously wondering what in the world these people were doing sitting in their apartment complex, but no one was coming out to us. Then, all of a sudden, a man walked out with a huge German shepherd. He walked over, scoped out the situation, and joined us when we told him what we were doing.

As he began to eat, it became clear that he was lonely. He told us that he had just moved to the area from Florida, and we all talked until it started to get dark. When he was about to leave, he said, "Hey, it seems like you've got a lot of soup left. Do you think I could take some of it to the guys I work with? I work in construction, and I think they would love it if I could take them some soup tomorrow."

Of course the answer was yes, and I ran to my house and grabbed every Tupperware container with a lid that I could find. We filled them all with soup and then helped carry it up to the man's door. When we arrived, it was obvious that he didn't want anyone to come in, but he gratefully accepted the soup and we said goodbye.

After he shut the door, my friend Mandy, who had been standing next to me, leaned over and said, "Ronda, there's nothing in there. That apartment is empty."

We all went back to my house and debriefed the evening. A few members of the group were focused on the numbers, and they were discouraged. And it's true—if we focused on the numbers, it was a huge failure. We only met one person. But the more we talked, the more we realized the opportunities we had with this one connection God had given us. We ultimately decided to give our new friend a collective "Welcome to Tennessee" housewarming gift.

The next Sunday, we knocked on the door to his apartment with our arms full of towels and bedding and basic groceries, and we officially welcomed him to the state. He looked at us in complete amazement and asked, "This is all for me?"

We assured him it was and told him how much we enjoyed getting to know him over a bowl of soup the previous week. Then, we gave him

Mandy and her husband's name and number and left. The next week, Mandy reported that he had called them, not to ask for anything for himself, but to see if we could do anything to help a single mom who lived in one of the other units. He worried that she didn't have enough money to feed her kids.

We reached out to her and eventually ended up buying her a car as a group. She then connected us to another neighbor, who connected us to another neighbor, and we kept saying yes to blessing our neighbors for as long as God kept opening doors. And it all started because we said yes to taking soup!

We can't figure out what God is going to do, and we can't possibly know the details of how things will unfold when we first set out. We really shouldn't even try to determine for ourselves what success looks like. Only one person showed up for soup, but it led to multiple opportunities to love and serve people in Jesus' name. But even when obedience doesn't lead to measurable results, success lies in the simple act of saying yes to God. He does the rest.

So when you feel a nudge from Him, don't question it to death. Don't allow yourself to become paralyzed by the unknowns. Just move forward in obedience. He will bring you further than you ever thought possible.

ONE TIME, God *literally* brought me further than I thought possible. He asked me to run a marathon. And, want to hear something crazier? I said yes. I couldn't have even told you why God had me training for a marathon until recently, but I'll take you on the journey with me before I explain.

Keep in mind, I, Ronda Paulson, am not a runner. I ran track in high school just to try to stay in shape, but I was awful at it. Like, guys I knew on my high school baseball team would be practicing at the same time as us on the track team, and they would make bets on whether I would pass out or fall. I was the worst runner. I've made my peace with that.

Now, at this point in time, I was in my early thirties, and the furthest I had run was a 5K Turkey Trot sponsored by the local YWCA. I ran it in a homemade shirt with the words "I hate running" printed on it, and I finished seventy-first out of seventy-two runners. The seventy-second person was my running partner.

Along the way, we were passed by an eighty-year-old woman and a young woman pushing a stroller. The YWCA van was right behind us, and at intersections they would call on a bullhorn to those manning the race route, "They're the last ones. Go ahead and clean it up." And the people would start picking up cones and sweeping the street as we passed. I even picked up a few cones, too, just to help them out.

After the race, we went to brunch with some friends, and I told them that I thought God was asking me to run a marathon. They all stared at me in disbelief. "Ronda, I think you heard that message wrong," said one of my friends. "You've run one race, and you came in dead last. Maybe work your way up to an 8K or 10K race before you try a marathon."

But I was sure. So I printed off a training schedule, and I read the plan for the first week. Three, three, six, three. Six miles! I had never run six miles in my life. I was a mother and a wife and a high school teacher and cheer coach —how was I supposed to make time for this, never mind my concerns about actually being able to complete the runs?

On my six-mile day, I was talking to some of my students about how I'd never run six miles, and one of my cheer girls said she would run it with me.

"Have you ever run six miles before?" I asked.

"No."

"Okay. Let's do it."

So that day, after school, we went and ran six miles. That was the push I needed to get going, and for the rest of my training I ran by myself. No music, no partner, just me and God.

When I got about halfway through the training, I was telling a friend that I didn't feel great the farther I got into my runs, and that around the ten-mile mark I would get dizzy.

"Well, are you drinking water?" she asked.

"Uhh, no," I told her. "Not on my runs."

"You're training for a marathon, and you're not hydrating at all?"

Clearly, I knew nothing at all about distance running. Once my friends realized that, they started meeting me on my long runs with water and Gatorade. And I just kept putting on my running shoes every day, following my little print-out schedule.

Even with help from friends, the training process was far from easy. On one of my runs, I was crying as I ran through the middle of our town. I was over it. In my head—because I had no extra breath to use for talking out loud—I was yelling at God. Because honestly, what was the point of this? He knew I wasn't a runner. He knew what He was asking of me when He said to do this. So, why? I hated it.

But every time I almost quit, something would happen to make me keep going. That day, when I was at the height of my exhaustion, a little blue Ford Fiesta passed by, and the driver honked and yelled, "You can do it!" Somehow, that was all I needed to keep going, and I thanked the Lord and continued.

Another time, I was halfway up a hill that could have rivaled the infamous Sutton Hill, and I told God, "You know what? I'm done. This is the dumbest thing. Take soup—I can do that.

Teach step aerobics—sure. But this? I can't anymore."

I saw a nice, ranch-style house nearby and I said to God, "Do you see that house over there? I'm going to walk over there and use their phone, and I'm going to call somebody to come get me."

I walked over and knocked on the door, and a young girl answered. Since this was still the era before we all just carried cell phones around, I asked to use their phone. She responded in the way her parents probably taught her to answer a stranger at their front door by saying, "We don't have one," and then shutting the door in my face.

Okay. New plan. "Fine, Lord, I don't need a phone. I'm just going to catch a ride with the next person who's willing to pick me up." As I walked to the road, a big, dirty Chevy Blazer slowed down for me, and I thought, *Okay, yeah, I am not getting in that car.* So, with no other options, I finished my run.

Hours and hours of training for that marathon were spent talking to God. When I couldn't go anymore, I would walk and sing "There's Power in the Blood" as loudly as my lungs would allow. Training for that marathon was one of the hardest things I've ever done. All I knew was that God had asked me to do it, so there I was.

When the race day finally came, I was surprised to find that it was such a fun experience. People stood all along the route with signs and music and encouragement, and those five hours and thirty-five minutes went by faster than I expected.

During the race I was reminded, once again, of God's sense of humor. Seriously, He could hardly have called me to a more foreign world than the world of running. For example, one thing I didn't know about beforehand were the stops along the way labeled as gel stations. I'd never heard of a gel station, and for the life of me I couldn't figure out what they were for.

When I arrived at the first station, I thought to myself, "Well, a gel sounds like something you would apply to what's hurting the most?" I decided it was my quads, opened the tube of gel, and rubbed it on my hands. I was just about to apply it when I noticed—to my shock—that everyone else was eating the gel. So, obviously, I did the only thing I could do at that moment. I gave the other runners a nod of "this is how I eat my gel" and began to lick my fingers.

Turns out the gel is a sugary substance used to give you energy on a long run. Who knew? I crossed the finish line of the Country Music Marathon in Nashville with God by my side and hands that felt like they'd been dipped in maple syrup. It was an incredible day.

For years I didn't understand why God had me run that marathon. But then, just like that, a few months ago it clicked. I told the Lord, "You wanted me to run that marathon so I could learn to hear Your voice. When I physically couldn't do it, You showed me that You were with me—and You still are. You provided for me, and You didn't let me quit. You proved to me that I can do so much more than I ever thought I could possibly achieve."

That marathon was something God used to increase my dependence on Him. To teach me a new level of trust. To show me what it looks like to literally dedicate each small step forward to Him.

As you can see, God has been working on my heart for *years*. And I am so grateful. Anything good that has come from my life is purely a testament to God's glory and goodness. The step aerobics, the soup, the running 26.2 miles, and everything in between—it's all Him. I just said yes. And, it turns out, all of this was just preparing me for my biggest yes yet.

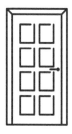

A Note from Sophie

WHEN ASKED what I first thought fostering and adoption would be like, I felt like I was not able to give the most accurate answer. I was only twelve, so I assumed I had forgotten a lot, but it's quite the opposite. I can tell you exactly what I remember feeling. I know without a doubt that there was no fear or hesitation, and I know I just felt the purest level of joy and excitement deep in my soul when my Daddy gave Momma and me the "yes."

That yes to me at the time just meant constant baby snuggles, and I don't think I can even put that twelve-year-old's level of excitement into words. My little heart could barely take it. I truly do not think anything else crossed my mind—not one negative thought, not even any questions on how this was going to play out (which is so off-brand for me, haha). I'm wound just about as tight as someone could be and quite literally have thirty-plus questions for every single thing that happens in a day. This was different though. Looking back, there was only gratitude, joy, and peace in my heart about all these babies I was going to potentially get to snuggle.

Now, at twenty years old and about eight years into this process, I feel like I can say so much more. I could tell you about the fears that showed up along the way when it felt like their sweet faces may be slipping through our fingertips while we were just told to watch and pray for protection. I could tell you about the stresses that were put on our family as we were these babies' first line of defense or about the pressures of being their only voice when they couldn't defend their own. I could tell you about so much, but there is too much beauty to waste time on fears or negatives. I actually don't even like to use the word "negatives" because I believe there aren't any to fostering or adopting. There are things you learn and things that shake up your normal, but I've yet to find one true "negative" eight years in.

One thing has shifted slightly from my twelve-year-old self. Her heart was so giddy about all the babies. I can assure you that my twenty-year-old heart is just as giddy about babies and about those boys, but I never knew the way Jesus would completely transform that little heart and form the woman I am today through fostering and adoption.

People would stop us to ask why or how we could take in two babies that weren't ours. Or they would tell us how nice it was of us but they couldn't ever do it in fear of having to give them back. Those comments stuck with me because I couldn't understand how people didn't see it. Jesus showed me so clearly why we were doing this. He led me hand in hand in a way that felt different from how others saw it. This is probably the first time it is in writing because it's something I can't quite accurately explain in words.

I know I can confidently say that Jesus moves so big in the trenches. He moves when we're in the mess and when our hearts are full of both fear and love. He moves when we move for Him. I believe with everything in me that these defenseless babies are near to our God's heart, and although stepping into something like fostering and adoption may seem too scary, He's moving. If we were scared to love, if we were scared of it being hard, where would my boys be today? Because we took that step, because we went out of our comfort zone, our boys are thriving. They are growing, loving, safe, and learning about Jesus, and I'm fully convinced nothing in this world beats that. This is the best of the land, God's love is the best of the land. Foster care might strike us with fear sometimes, or maybe adoption seems too far out of that comfort zone, but I can wholeheartedly say it truly is the best thing that has ever happened to me.

I often get the question, "Was it just as easy to love them as it was to love your bio brother?" or, "Is it harder because they aren't biological?" That question just baffles me, and I find myself almost getting offended by it. How could you just not fall madly in love with a baby? How does it not just completely overflow from every part of your body?! How could someone even ask that?

I truthfully never knew I could love two little humans so much. They taught me how to be compassionate and brave. They have the kindest souls, and they constantly show me that blood doesn't matter. I think everyone should live this life with Isaiah's level of joy and with Eli's kindness toward everyone he meets. They love so well. They love without boundaries just as Jesus teaches us to. I could make an entire list on all the ways Jesus is in them and the ways those babies brought Jesus to me, but I'll spare your time!

Adoption, foster care, those babies—they are the best, hardest thing we have ever done, and I'm forever thankful to know them. There aren't enough thank-yous in the world for those boys. There aren't enough thank-yous in this world for how adoption shaped me. I have the utmost gratitude for the most loving God who walks through adoption with each person willing to take the step. I'm overflowing with thanksgiving to Jesus for giving us the opportunity to serve His kingdom in such a mighty way. That I got to be and continue to be a part of something way beyond me. That He has made Himself so evident through this whole process in so many ways.

Chapter Five

I t was 2013, and I was knee-deep in the midst of everyday life. I was working as a lab instructor and cheer and dance coach, raising my family, and generally just trying to be faithful in the places where I knew to be faithful. But I was also on the lookout.

Corey and I had both been praying for God to reveal anything that He might have for us to do. We were praying for what was next, and we were ready to go all in. Surrender and obedience—those words were the steady theme of those days as we prayed that we would listen well to God.

One Thursday morning, I woke up sick and couldn't go into work. I got the kids off to school and immediately climbed back into bed and lay there, watching the *Today Show*. It was National Adoption Month, and the show that morning featured a judge performing one adoption after another, creating forever families right there on the plaza.

So, there I lay in bed, *crying*, because I was sick and I was tired and this was beautiful, and because how in the world had Corey and I not adopted already? And then I heard the TV host announce that 75 percent of the children adopted that day had come through the foster care system.

On that Thursday morning in 2013, I knew nothing about foster care, nor did I know anyone who had walked that path. But something about it captured my attention, and I grabbed my laptop and googled "foster care in Northeast Tennessee."

The first thing that came up were classes for people wanting to become certified foster parents. It was an eight-week course, and the classes were starting the following Thursday at a church Corey and I were familiar with. Timing like that when you're praying for God to reveal next steps does not feel like a coincidence.

Corey had been a great sport about so many of my adventures for as long as I had known him, but adoption was something we'd never seriously considered together. I can remember countless "Orphan Sunday" sermons in which a minister would play a horrible video about a child not being chosen. I would be under the pew, doing the ugly cry—but not Corey. He would just look at me and say, "Ronda, get up! People are looking at you!" He did not want to talk about it, think about it, or pray about it. But maybe if I could just get him to these classes . . . maybe then he would change his mind.

So, I did the only thing a God-loving, passionate woman could do. I called my husband at work and asked, "Want to go on a date?"

The following Thursday, we went to dinner at one of our favorite places. As we were leaving, I decided it was time to speak up or give up, so I said, "I want to drive out to Crossroads Christian Church."

He turned to me and asked, "On our date?"

"Yeah." He looked over at me, knowing something was up, so I added innocently, "Let's just go see what's happening, you know?"

We drove the fifteen minutes to Crossroads Christian Church, and as we pulled into the parking lot Corey noticed that several other cars were already there.

"Looks like there are a lot of people datin' at the Crossroads Christian Church," he said dryly.

We still joke today about what his first thoughts were as we parked. He probably thought he was being ambushed, that he'd been tricked into marital counseling or something. And I guess that's not totally wrong. But he definitely couldn't have guessed what I'd actually gotten us into.

We sat down inside, and a woman opened the meeting. "Welcome to your eight-week study of foster care!"

Corey began to stare me down, *not* happy, and I chose not to engage with him at that moment. Sometimes it's better to just smile and avoid eye contact.

At the end of the night, we got in our car and did not say a word about anything that we had learned. We drove home in silence, and then the next morning got up and acted like nothing had happened. Then, the following Thursday, without any discussion, we met up in the driveway, got in the car, and went to week two.

This continued through week three. On the way home from the third class, Corey finally spoke up.

"I don't want to do this," he said.

"Fair enough," I said. "I mean, you've been a good sport, and we made it three weeks. I tricked you into it to begin with. Fair enough."

But he responded, "Oh, don't 'fair enough' me, Ronda."

"What?"

"You and the Lord have wrecked me with this," he went on. "You know me, I like simple and safe and predictable. And nothing that we have learned about foster care in the last three weeks sounds simple or safe or predictable. And I do not want to do this. But now I know the numbers. I know the statistics. Now I know that there are children in our county who don't have a home. And we *have* to do this."

That was the turning point for us as a couple. We were in this. Together. Called by God out of our comfort zone and into an undeniable directive to *obey*.

WE WENT BACK for week four, and then for weeks five through eight. For our seventh class, they took us on a field trip to the Department of Children's Services office in Washington County, Tennessee—right down the road from where we lived.

It was the first time I'd ever been in a DCS office. I've since been to countless DCS offices, and I can personally attest to the fact that if you've seen one DCS office, you've seen them all. Tile floors, a vending machine in the lobby, fluorescent lights. A maze of cubicles and conference rooms.

Our group sat down in one of the conference rooms, and a lawyer began leading the class. I don't remember anything he talked about—

except for one thing. He said, "When a child is removed from their home, they come here."

I took a closer look around the conference room. No windows. Cold. Sterile. Carpet that looked thin and worn. State-issued furniture. Phones that still plugged into the wall. Everything drab and gray. Surely I had heard him wrong. *Why would you ever bring a child into this room?* I raised my hand.

"I'm sorry, but when you say a child comes here, what exactly do you mean?" I asked.

His response broke my heart.

"A little girl slept on this floor last night."

My mind formed a picture of a little girl, age six or seven, who had just left the only momma she'd ever known. And although we might not approve, she did. She now found herself completely alone with all her earthly belongings —if she had any—in a black trash bag, and she was sleeping on this dirty carpet all by herself. I couldn't shake the feeling of how lonely and scary it must have been for her. I also couldn't shake the question accompanying the pang in my chest: *How could this be the plan?*

The desperate sadness of it all filled me with anger. But I wasn't angry at the parents or the case managers—not even at the broken system. I was mad at God. The conference room and the lawyer's voice faded away as I retreated within myself and began to have it out with God.

In my head, I yelled from a place of deep confusion and despair, "This little girl is *yours*. And she was left *here*—on this floor, all alone, on one of her worst days. Who's going to tell her that she's not alone? Who's going to tell her that she's beautiful and that there is hope and that she has a future to look forward to? This is one of the most terrifying and vulnerable days of her life— who's going to tell her that she's loved?"

Of course, I wasn't angry simply because a little girl had spent the night in that conference room. I was angry because of all that that fact represented. In a whole new way, it hit me: this world is so broken. And that brokenness extends even to our children.

This little girl had done nothing to deserve a life of uncertainty, abuse, or abandonment. She had done nothing to deserve to be born to parents who, for whatever reason, couldn't care for her.

And yet, that had been her experience. It was her experience right now. She was somewhere in the county in a foster home that was hopefully safe and healing for her. But regardless, she was still dealing with the fact that life as she knew it had been turned upside down.

At that very moment, as I stood there in that conference room, she was learning to cope, even if she didn't realize it. Was she choosing to harden herself, to protect herself from future pain by numbing herself to the present hurt? Was she angry and lashing out, keeping everyone at arm's length to ensure she would never be hurt again, not understanding she was making it that much harder for her to receive love? Was she latching on to anyone who looked her way, desperately seeking attention and approval from anyone who would offer it? Was she crying uncontrollably, or not crying at all, or was she shutting down altogether?

My heart cried out—to her, for her, on her behalf. This is not fair! She has done nothing wrong! There has to be a better way.

All these thoughts, accusations, and questions washed over me in the span of a couple seconds, but they flooded my mind and clouded out all light. Everything felt so hopeless; every problem felt so pressing. Standing in the conference room, my shoulders bent beneath the weight.

But then I heard Him. I heard the Lord's voice as I had heard Him many times before. Deep in my spirit, I heard Him, felt Him, knew He was there. I heard God say, "These are my children. What are you going to do?"

I froze. What had felt like a rescue light in a storm suddenly felt like an unwelcome spotlight shining right in my face as I realized the implications of what God had said to me. I was already moving toward an unknown by saying yes to fostering, and God was asking me to go further? To do more?

No, no, no. I was just there for the classes. I was a cheer and dance coach, and this was a broken foster-care system. What was I supposed to do against an entire system? This was a problem so big that only God could fix it—at a heavenly level or something.

I left that conference room, and I did not tell a soul what God had told me for another two and a half years. I could hardly even acknowledge it to myself. How could God be asking for more when we were already doing so much to take in even one child?

We finished the foster-care course, and then went back to life as normal. That is, we went back to life as normal after moving houses and switching cars. The historic farmhouse we had been in was too small and didn't have room for another child, so we sold it and moved into a more spacious house in town. Around the same time in the spring of 2014, we also traded our car in for a minivan, which I still believe was my biggest sacrifice up to that point.

It took until the fall of 2014 to become officially licensed to accept foster children. And after that, it was almost a year before a placement came along that was right for our family. However, Corey and I had become friends with others who were part of the class. As they received placements, we heard more and more stories about what it looked like for a child to be officially moved from one home to another through the system.

One friend of mine, Julie, whom I'd met through the course, got a call in the same week after completing our course to take in a newborn who was exposed to drugs. She went to pick him up at the hospital, and he literally had nothing. She didn't even have to show an ID before she was allowed to take him with her.

She called me frequently over the next several weeks to vent about what was going on. She saw, up close and early on, the incredible sadness that comes with caring for a baby with his story. She told me of their issues with fulfilling the required visitations with the baby's abusive father, and of their struggles with calming down an infant who had been exposed to drugs so early. She told me of how long, lonely, and uncertain it felt to foster.

These stories from her and others filled my thoughts as I continued in my everyday life. Mostly, I couldn't let go of the fact that children had so little say in what happened to them, and that, on one of the worst days of their life, they often ended up waiting alone for hours in a well-meaning but under-resourced office. Clearly, there were pressing needs in foster care. Clearly, it was a heavy and difficult world to be a part of. But *clearly*, a messy situation or a hard reality is not a reason to tap out, but rather to lean further in.

ON NOVEMBER 5, we said yes to Isaiah. I got to see for myself how true everything I'd heard about fostering really was. Yep, the kids often come with nothing. Yep, there is hardly any preparation or background information available for the foster family that's taking them in. And yep, even with community support, foster care feels isolating and tiring, and you feel ill-equipped and overwhelmed.

From the fall of 2015 to the summer of 2018, I was in the DCS office every Friday morning from ten to noon for visitation with Isaiah's (and eventually Eli's) biological mom. I often tell people that I didn't learn the inner workings of foster care, the DCS office, or the "system" from a video or a church pew; I learned it by being there.

I learned it by sitting in that waiting room. I met caseworkers and learned how hard their job truly is, how many hours they work, how little they're paid, and how underappreciated they are.

I learned it through the receptionist, Darlene, who saw the good, the bad, and the ugly sides of me. Over those years of Fridays, she saw me crash, cuss, laugh, cry, and try not to fall asleep in that waiting room. She also taught me what it looks like to navigate the world of foster care.

I also learned it by walking through the visitation space. It's a tiny room with a dirty two-way mirror. Kids' belongings sit in an adjoining room, haphazardly shoved into cubicles so they can keep everything together while they wait to leave.

All through 2016, I kept saying no to anything beyond caring for Isaiah, but it was becoming increasingly obvious to me God was still calling me to more. And, as I got to know the DCS office and the specific people involved—Isaiah, his mom, Darlene, the caseworkers, Julie—I slowly began to see places where more could be done. I couldn't fix the entire system, but maybe there were a few practical needs that could be met, with the help of God, by someone as ordinary as me.

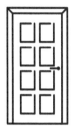

A Story from the House

I REMEMBER *the first time we got a call for a sibling group. There were five siblings, all fourteen and under. When they arrived, me, two other volunteers, and two caseworkers were already there waiting to receive them. We'd been told that the oldest was on the way to the emergency room to be checked out and that she would be joining us later.*

The first thing that struck me about this group of kids was that the boys were my son's age. I kept looking at them and thinking, Do you go to school with Mac? Do you play soccer with him? Have I met your parents? They were your typical rambunctious boys; we played darts and basketball and remote-control cars and got out some of their energy.

The toddler was very excited to see the craft table, and she sat there for a long time with a sweet volunteer. They colored, glittered, and glued, and I'm pretty sure slime was made.

The baby could not be comforted. At first we couldn't figure out why, but then we started to realize that he was trying to nuzzle in. He wanted to breastfeed but didn't have his momma. I walked and rocked and walked and rocked and finally got him to sleep in my arms. And about the time he fell asleep, the oldest sister got back from the hospital.

Her face had been beaten. Not just a black eye or a bruise on the cheek—her entire face. I later found out that that was how they came into state custody; a neighbor saw her outside and called the police.

We all worked hard to keep our expressions in check as we greeted her with a warm welcome.

Before she got there, the two older boys had taken charge of the littles. They were telling us what the younger ones liked and what they would eat and wouldn't eat. It's a pattern that we have come to expect with sibling sets. The oldest always takes care of the youngest.

As we were finishing up getting everyone bathed and fed and packed, we got word that placement had been found. They were all going to live with their 80-year-old grandmother. I remember thinking that night that if those five kids just wore me and four other capable adults out, what in the world is Grandma going to do?

That night a new understanding of the purpose of an Isaiah 117 House dawned on me. We weren't just caring for the children on their way to a foster home. We were caring for the children on their way to a facility, and we were absolutely caring for the children on their way to another family member.

So, we reached out to Grandma to see what she needed. She did not have enough beds, so we got beds and bedding and food and clothes and connected her with everyone she might need for the coming days. When the kids left that night, the two volunteers and I fell onto the couch, exhausted from physical activity, exhausted from the emotional stress of seeing that kind of abuse firsthand, and exhausted for Grandma and for what she had said yes to.

The next morning, I was sitting in church when I got a message on Facebook. A lady I did not know said, "I don't know if you can confirm this or not, but I think five kids from my church were at the Isaiah 117 House last night. I've taught them in Sunday School for years, and we had no idea."

Chapter Six

It seemed like the Lord was asking me to make space in my life for something He wanted to do, and, although I didn't know what it would be, I was ready to say yes. In late 2016, I went to my boss and asked him if I could go part-time. We can't always know what's coming, but we can still prepare faithfully.

After getting that approved, the only thing I knew to do was to set up a meeting with Julie. So, one afternoon in January of 2017, I walked into a local coffee shop with the Yes Prayer on my heart. We sat across from one another, talking about needs in the foster care system, specifically in regard to removal day. We tried to think about it from all angles—the needs of the child, the parents, the caseworkers. And an idea began to emerge.

What if there was a home? A place where the kids would be intentionally and specifically cared for while they waited? What could it look like? What would we call it?

Sitting there in that coffee shop, we googled "how to start a nonprofit," and a few minutes later, we ordered a book on Amazon called *Nonprofits for Dummies*. If that doesn't tell you how little we knew about what we were getting into, I don't know what will.

If you want God to have the glory, you put someone totally unequipped in charge. And that's exactly what He did.

The name Isaiah 117 House was one I'd been thinking about for a while. Corey had first seen that verse on a shirt somewhere and had pointed it out to me. We went back and read Isaiah 1:17, which says, "Learn to do right; seek justice. Defend the oppressed. Take up the cause of the fatherless; plead the case of the widow." That's a verse that hits you pretty hard when you're staring at a child, defenseless and dependent, who literally has nothing.

Some context may help further explain why this verse was so important to me. In the first chapter of Isaiah, God is speaking to His people, and He's actually quite frustrated. His people are offering sacrifices to Him, but they aren't the sacrifices He desires. Israel wanted to sacrifice to God on their own terms, but in doing what they thought was appropriate, they strayed further from what God had asked of them. God reminds them what He's truly after, and that's when he gets to the commands in verse 17.

So, Corey and I had already adopted Isaiah 1:17 as a kind of family mission statement. And, as I kept thinking about a potential home for removal day, I couldn't shake an image of a white house with a red door. In this image, it was Christmas, and every passerby could see a beautiful, colorful Christmas tree through the picture window in the front. And under the tree was a present labeled by name for each child who entered.

Sitting in that coffee shop, we knew the name for the nonprofit couldn't be anything except Isaiah 117 House.

We bought the domain name then and there. To be clear, I didn't know what a domain name was, and I still don't understand who GoDaddy is, but I did learn that if you give them your credit card, they'll give you a name. We had a dot com! And I had further direction.

I set up a meeting with Pam Harr, the team coordinator for the local DCS office, and officially pitched this idea for the first time. As I cast the vision for her, explaining how we could serve both the children and adults whose lives are affected by the foster system, her eyes filled with tears.

She had been working at that office for thirty-six years, but you would have thought she'd started work there yesterday because of how soft her heart still was. She should have been jaded and bitter. She should have told me it could never work after watching other initiatives flop. She should have turned me away after working for so long within a system that is as discouraging as it is cyclical. But instead, as I finished speaking and leaned back in my chair, she looked at me and said, "Let's try."

Let's try. May my responses to others consistently be as faith-filled as hers.

Pam recommended that I reach out to a lady named Joni Cannon, who was already running a nonprofit ministry for foster children called Cap the Gap. I promised to reach out to her and then thanked Pam and said goodbye.

Feeling confident, I stopped at Darlene's receptionist desk on my way out and told her my dream. She, too, was incredibly supportive, and immediately suggested that I talk to a woman named Joni Cannon because she would absolutely love the idea.

Then, as Darlene was still talking, she focused on someone coming in the front door behind me and said, "Oh, well, there's Joni Cannon."

Obviously, God wasn't wasting any time with this, so I decided I wouldn't either. I introduced myself to Joni Cannon, and right then and there, in the DCS lobby, I told her about our idea for Isaiah 117 House.

As we talked, she kept repeating, "A house! I love this idea. I never dreamed of having a house." We promptly planned a meeting for later that week.

As I got in my car, I wondered whether we could raise money under her 501(c)(3) until we could get one of our own. But I shut that thought down pretty quickly because I was afraid it broke a personal rule of mine that I like to call, "Don't Be Too Pushy Because for Heaven's Sake You Just Met this Person, Ronda."

Here I was, thinking I'd ask if I could use her nonprofit to collect money for mine, and I had met this sweet woman twenty minutes ago. Like, seriously? On top of that, we couldn't actually become part of her 501(c)(3) because we'd need to stay separate in order to form our own board and offer salaried positions one day. So it would likely be a big complication for her to take on, and in order to actually make Isaiah 117 House happen, I had to be realistic. Asking Joni for help in that particular way was not realistic. How would that conversation even go? I would have to think of something else.

We met up for coffee a few days later, and Joni brought a legal pad with notes written down for our conversation. As we sat down, I caught a glimpse of the top page. On it, her first point said, "Use Cap the Gap as an umbrella and 501(c)(3) for Isaiah 117 House." Her second point was something like, "Eventually, they will come out from under us so they can offer salaried positions and have their own board."

I sat very still with my coffee and tried to act like a person who does not read other people's notes, and she started us off.

"My daughter is a lawyer, and I first want to say that I talked to her and she feels good about us using Cap the Gap as an umbrella nonprofit for you so that you can begin taking donations immediately," she explained. "And then the second thing I keep thinking is that you should be your own separate thing within our 501(c)(3) because you'll want to have your own as soon as you can."

Sitting in that coffee shop and listening as Joni talked through more details (that I hadn't had a chance to read off her notepad), I cried at the tangible goodness of God.

"I've got a lawyer who did our nonprofit paperwork for free, and I'm sure he'd do the same thing for you, too," she went on. "I'll connect you with him."

I left that meeting with everything I needed to get our 501(c)(3) up and running—and with incredible resources that would help us start getting traction immediately. I began praying about board members for Isaiah 117 House, and we had our first board meeting on February 26, 2017.

THE DREAM TOOK shape in that first board meeting. We had our goal: to have a home. With that home, we would reduce trauma for children, lighten the load of case managers, and ease the transition for future placements. A secondary but equally important goal was to raise the money to pay cash for the house. We didn't want any debt holding us back.

The new question became, how do we fundraise for something like that? I met with a friend of mine named Joy who had done things like that before, and as I told her the vision and our current predicament, she started to laugh. A little surprised, I asked her if she was laughing at my dream.

"No, Ronda," she replied. "I'm laughing because you think there's only going to be one house. That's what's so funny to me."

Joy is the one who gets the credit for my "Sundays with Ronda" videos. She told me to go home and start recording myself on my phone once a week, just talking about whatever was going on. She said, "I'm going to set up a Facebook account for you."

"But I don't want the Facebook."

She good-naturedly put up with my pushback. "Ronda, I'm setting up 'the Facebook.' Do you want the house? You'll need 'the Facebook.'"

I caved, and Joy called me a couple days later, gave me the login to my brand-new Facebook page, and told me to figure out how to use it. I tried one more time to slow down the Facebook idea, but she came back with:

"The video I posted of you and Corey has gotten 25,000 views, and the local news would like to interview you. Figure. Out. The. Facebook."

That's what I did. I figured out the Facebook.

I'm telling you, the power of the like and share!

Suddenly I couldn't go anywhere in our community without someone stopping me. Usually it was a big burly man, saying "My wife made me watch that video. It had me crying in my coffee. We gotta get them kids a house."

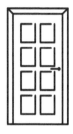

A Note From Mac

WHEN THE IDEA TO foster first came about, I cannot say I was very excited. It had always been me and Sophie; it had always been routine and predictable. So, I was not psyched about the idea. Keep in mind, I was only eight years old at the time. Also, I was the baby of the family (the "fan favorite," some might say).

Bringing in a new baby would take the attention away from me and give it all to the kid, and I didn't like the sound of that. But as they say, you can't say you don't like something until you try it, so I was hoping this would be a great learning experience for everyone.

When the words were first said, "If your last name is Paulson, get in the van," I didn't want to move. I was in denial. I've never liked change, and this was no small change at all.

But this change was better than I expected. It only took me about two weeks to settle in and become comfortable with this new kid that we picked up from the back of a DCS office. Adopting not one but two children has changed this family for the better. It has most definitely pulled this family closer together, no matter how many struggles we've all faced when it has come to taking care of these kids that I now get to call my brothers. All in all, it has helped my life in so many ways by providing me with opportunities to love unconditionally and be more like Jesus.

Chapter Seven

I t's more or less known that most work in the nonprofit world is fundraising, raising awareness, and fundraising some more. That aspect of nonprofit work characterized 2017 for me more than any other year. Every interview, every speaking engagement, every connection mattered. I just kept walking through the doors God opened.

Very few of the avenues God provided for fundraising were due to our own strategic efforts; most materialized in unexpected ways. In fact, one of our biggest sources of revenue wasn't something we sought out at all.

One day, sitting in a church pew and casually catching up with a good friend of mine, I mentioned that I wanted to create some Isaiah 117 House T-shirts to give as a gift to our board members. And, because we at Isaiah 117 House are an incredibly high-tech organization (insert sarcasm), she kindly offered to set up her personal Cricut and make them herself.

Still sitting in that church pew, we ordered blank T-shirts and decided with Corey to put "Love, You're Not Alone" on the front and the Isaiah 117 House logo on the back.

She made exactly twelve shirts on her kitchen counter with that Cricut for the ten board members, Corey, and me. We loved them, and I decided to post a picture on the Facebook of Corey wearing his. Before I hit post, I had a fleeting thought wondering whether people would think we were selling them. I wasn't sure, and Corey didn't think so. I posted.

We had 100 orders in 30 minutes.

Joy, my marketing extraordinaire, called me as soon as she saw the post and said, "Please tell me you're not selling T-shirts out of the back of your van."

She didn't even know the half of it. "Oh no, Joy, I can one-up you. There are no T-shirts."

"Um, what?"

"There are no T-shirts."

"But you have 100 orders."

"Yeah, but we aren't selling them."

"Well," she laughed, "You are now."

That day, Joy set up a GoFundMe account to let people "donate" twenty bucks so I could drive a shirt to their house. I was literally selling shirts out of the back of my van.

In those days (and, I have to tell you, not much has changed), I was traveling and talking to anyone who would listen about the need for the Isaiah 117 House. I followed any lead I received, and throughout 2017, I spoke in more churches and civic organizations than I can remember as I sought to raise awareness and funds for this dream I'd been given.

At one of my speaking engagements, I ran into one of my Milligan coworkers, who had also become a friend and mentor. I told him my dream, including the fact that we were still looking for a house.

He stopped me and said, "We're looking to sell our house. We haven't put it on the market yet."

I was excited but also hesitant. I felt like God had told me to budget $75,000 for a house, and there was no way he would sell his house at such a low price. I asked him how much they were planning to ask for it, and sure enough, he told me a number that was more than double that amount.

"Listen, we're only going to pay $75,000," I said. "I'm not saying you should sell it to me for that much because I realize that's such a significant price difference, but that's why we probably can't buy from you."

He nodded in understanding, and we finished catching up and parted ways.

The next day came, and with it, a phone call. "My wife and I prayed about it, and if this house will work for you, we want to sell it to you for $75,000."

He gave me the address, and I drove out there right away. As soon as I pulled into the driveway I knew we had found our house.

It was exactly what I had been seeing in my mind for months. White house. Red door. Big picture window in the front.

I just had one thing to say to these kind, generous friends: "Sold."

Now, it's important to note that all of this happened before we had any money. We definitely didn't have $75,000, and at that point in the summer of 2017, we were still in the critical stages of raising awareness and support to make this a reality that would actually help people.

But, once again, God was one step ahead of us. Without any prompting from us, kids throughout Northeast Tennessee began selling lemonade with the help of their parents, because they had heard there were other kids who needed a home and wanted to help.

Those lemonade stands brought in $7,000 that summer. It's since become an Isaiah 117 House tradition. Every year around mid-July, we have something called the Lemonade Stand Challenge Weekend. During the challenge weekend in July 2022, Isaiah 117 House held 650 stands and brought in $400,000. Since 2017, we've also sold over $1 million worth of T-shirts that we never meant to start selling. Only God.

IN AUGUST OF 2017, we put on one more event to get us to the finish line on raising the rest of the money we needed. After the event, I received a call from a man who had been in attendance.

"How much more money do you need?" he asked.

"We're short $5,000," I said.

He told me it would be no problem for him to send us a check for that amount on that day. When I hung up the phone, I sat for a moment, soaking in the fullness of God's provision. We had done it—the Isaiah 117 House could finally be purchased. God provided one dollar at a time through cups of lemonade, homemade T-shirts, and the hearts of generous, generous people eager to say yes to God.

A month later, we had the keys and were ready to move forward with inspections. Unfortunately, those inspections were proving to be more costly than we had hoped. The house had been built in 1940, and quite a bit of work was still needed to bring it up to code.

It seemed like each inspection brought more bad news. The house needed to be more open, which required that we remove quite a few walls, several of which were load-bearing. The house also had foundation issues, as the seller had already told me.

I had envisioned bringing in youth groups and volunteers to fix up the house for free. I would invite anyone and everyone to grab a paint-brush, put lipstick on this pig, and help us open a home to serve children. But not just anyone can remove every load-bearing wall on the first floor of a house with foundational issues. All of a sudden, I was having meetings with the code department and zoning and different contractors in the area. With every conversation, the question grew more pressing: How are we supposed to pay for this? We had just spent all our money purchasing the home. We didn't have more left over for extensive repairs.

So, I called a friend of mine. Well, maybe the word "friend" is misleading because I didn't really know him at all. He was the brother of a friend of mine, a contractor, and in that week, something else: my last hope. I asked him to come see the house.

We walked through the house and I asked him, "Do you think you could fix this?" And then I added, "For free?"

And then I found out what God already knew. This new friend had just been hired by the largest contracting firm in a nearby city, and a few days later I found myself in their board-room, pitching the mission of Isaiah 117 House and asking for their help. Above and beyond our hopes, they said that if we could get the house demoed to the studs within the next five days to meet their construction plan, they would rebuild all of it for free. New foundation, new walls, new roof, new windows, new plumbing, new electric—that sounded like something we could afford!

I took our request to another new friend of mine, the Facebook. I think that post said some-thing along the lines of, "Bring your children, bring your sledgehammers, come on out and let's demo this house." Anyway, whatever it said, it was questionable because our insurance guy called me five minutes after the post went up.

"Ronda, did you just publicly invite both children and sledgehammers to an uninsured home?"

Whoops. "Um, yes. Yes, I did."

He said, "I'm on it," then spent the rest of those five days making sure that he had insurance to cover anybody who might get hurt at the worksite, while I kept busy trying to get people to actually come to the worksite in the first place.

Firefighters, youth groups, families, friends, baseball teams, and small group members came at all times of the day and night over those few days, and we got the house gutted. Then, the contracting company came in and did $90,000 worth of work on that home. They never charged us a dime.

In the middle of that process, another group offered to fix up our entire backyard, worth $13,000, for free. They raised a privacy fence and built us a pavilion and play area. They painted our porch, did our landscaping, and hand-painted Dr. Seuss signs all around the yard.

The sign right outside the kitchen window resonates with me the most. It's a picture of Horton the Elephant with the famous quote, "A person's a person, no matter how small." Every time I see it I'm encouraged, because that's the whole point, isn't it?

You matter. Every child matters. A person's a person, and it's our job to care for each other.

One day as renovations on the house finished up, Cannon's Fine Home Furnishings, a local furniture company, came by. The owners, a father and son, walked through the house, writing measurements down on a notepad and talking quietly between themselves. When they finished, they came up to me and said, "Okay, we're going to order all of the furniture for the house."

I was overwhelmed with gratitude, but I was learning not to be surprised. God will provide for His children. They furnished the whole house, spending thousands of dollars to love on the children who would pass through those rooms.

Only one room was left untouched—the boys' room. That room had already been claimed by the firefighters who had helped to demo the house. On the day of the reveal, they unveiled the cutest firefighter-themed room you've ever seen. When they showed it to me, they handed me a plaque to put on the wall. It had their emblem in the middle, along with a verse from Isaiah, saying, "They will walk through fire, but they will not be burned" (Isaiah 43:2).

Overwhelmed by the goodness of it all, I started crying. Like, the ugly cry. But I quickly felt better about that because the firefighter who was handing me the plaque also started crying. It was the ugly cry for him, too. So, we were both just standing there, crying together, until he was finally able to gesture toward a firefighter standing several feet away and get out the words, "Well, you know Mike, he ordered that plaque off of Pinterest."

At that, we both began to laugh through our tears. To me, hearing that Firefighter Mike had been on Pinterest trying to find the perfect plaque for this house brought it all home for me. The entire community had rallied behind this project. The Lord had blessed it; it had been His since the beginning. It wasn't up to me to hold it all together or rally people to the cause. He would see it through, and He would put it on the hearts of His people to bring what they could. And it would be enough and more than enough, because God is enough and more than enough.

The Lord continued to provide. A weekly car show that runs throughout the summer gave us money; local nursing home residents did a bake sale to support us; churches and civic centers and schools contributed. Teachers came to help us decorate on their days off because they knew some of their students would be coming there. Our goal was $75,000 total. At the end of 2017, our board treasurer called me and said, "Ronda, we've received over $75,000 in December alone."

By the time we were ready to open our doors, our first year's budget was sitting in the bank. We had a debt-free home. Every closet was full of clothes, every cabinet was stocked. We had food, backpacks with school supplies, stuffed animals, blankets, toys, and movies. We had forty trained volunteers. We'd received the green light from the state. It was time.

IN THE MIDST of all of this, I got a call about a guy who was apparently running for governor in Tennessee. He and his team wanted to meet me. Now, the last thing I wanted was for Isaiah 117 House to be an easy photo-op for a politician whose platform I didn't even know, so at first I said no.

But, I had a few friends who knew him and his team and who basically gave me no choice other than to agree. So, a few days later, a guy named Bill Lee and his wife Maria showed up at the Carter County House. The house was still very much under construction, and I didn't even ask the guys to stop hammering when I greeted them outside.

We could barely hear each other because it was so loud. I did hear him tell me, however, that his entire platform was based on faith, and if a faith-based organization was doing really good work, why wouldn't the state want to work with them? He believed that our nonprofit was a great example, which caught my attention since our main concern at that point was what our working relationship with the state would look like.

Toward the end of our conversation, Bill Lee looked at me and asked, "So, what would you want Nashville to know?"

I was ready for that question. I told him about how the state has forgotten the children, how the child welfare system wasn't set up for the well-being of the child. I told him the reason behind building a house. I told him that without a house, children have to stay in cubicles for hours or days until a placement can be found for them. I told him the things that God had burdened me with and the mission He had given me, and by the time I finished, we all had tears in our eyes.

All of a sudden he said, "Can I pray for you?" There were no cameras, no one around to make it into a story for his benefit. And we stood there and we prayed for the children of Tennessee and for foster care.

In case you're wondering, yes, I did end up taking a picture with Bill Lee and Maria. My friends were right about me needing to meet them.

Bill Lee ended up becoming the governor of Tennessee, and in the process of his campaign he traveled all across the state, using Isaiah 117 House as a model for how the church and state can work together in a healthy way.

The timing couldn't have been better. At the exact time that we were needing to ensure that we could work hand-in-hand with the state, we had someone from the state cheering us on and championing us to everyone else. God continued to pave the way for us.

On ribbon-cutting day, I told the miraculous story of the Isaiah 117 House to all of the contractors and subcontractors we had invited to see the final result. I told them where the idea for the house began and shared how God had provided at every step of the way.

I hadn't realized it, but most of the men had said yes to the project because their boss had told them to. They didn't know why they were hanging drywall or landscaping the yard. It was just another project to them—until I told them the story.

When I got done, people walked up to me, one after another and some with tears in their eyes, saying, "When you do the next house, I want to be part of it."

The whole time I was thinking, *"This is amazing, but there is no next house. There already is a house and we're standing in it and now we're done."* I look back now and think that God must have been laughing and shaking His head at me. Little did I know how much more He had planned!

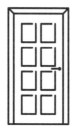

A Story from the House

I REMEMBER *the first time Pam Harr called me and said, "We have a teenage boy, and he's a runner."*

"Pam, please tell me this is a code for something."

"Yes, it is," she responded. "It's code for: he runs."

I was sitting at the dining room table of the Carter County House, looking at the front door. Although I am honestly pretty fast for my stature and freakishly strong—two of my favorite claims to fame, I thought—it was pushing it to think I could stop a fifteen-year-old boy if he decided to run out the front door. And if he were to run out that front door and into the road and get hit by a car, all of a sudden we're no longer Isaiah 117 House, the place that reduces trauma for children; we are that ministry that used to have some house before a kid ran out the front door and got run over. Simply put, we could not afford to have a kid run away from the house.

I told my thoughts to Pam. She got quiet for a minute and then said, gently, "Ronda, he just really needs a shower."

That was all I needed to put my concerns aside. "Oh, bring him, Pam." Within half an hour, a very large fifteen-year-old male stood in the kitchen with me. I welcomed him and said, "I want you to make yourself at home. This house is for you. And anything you see in that kitchen that you want to eat is yours."

He looked shocked, and I reassured him, "Go for it! Anything you see in any cabinet, freezer, or refrigerator that you want to eat is yours. Or if you can think of anything you want me to make you or order for you, it's yours. Whatever you want to eat."

He ate for the next hour and a half. When he left, I found that he had hidden food upstairs in one of the bedrooms. I get it—if you don't know where your next meal is coming from, you plan ahead.

After he ate, he took a shower, put on a pair of big, comfy, flannel pajama pants and a T-shirt, laid on the couch, and turned on some sports. I remember looking at him and thinking, I don't think he's going to run today.

Later on, I told that story to one of the firefighters who had helped with the house and still periodically stopped by. He responded, "Ronda, nobody runs from a place where they feel safe. He felt safe, and he stayed."

And that right there is the beauty of the Isaiah 117 House. It's hard to feel safe when you're sitting in a state office, but if you can be in a home, where there is a hot shower and you can eat and laugh with some crazy woman you just met, and you can put on brand new pajama pants and settle into a couch, chances are you'll feel pretty safe. There's not much to run from in that moment.

Chapter Eight

I kept believing for a while longer that this was a one-off house. God had rallied His people, and we had seen a small-town miracle. It was beautiful and an important service for Carter County, Tennessee, but it wasn't something we were going to repeat.

Yet, more and more people kept taking notice of the house . . . because it was *working*. I kept expressing my surprise, and those who heard me always said some version of, "Well, yeah, you told us it would." My response was always, "Yeah, but I didn't *know* if it would. I still can hardly believe you crazy people listen to me and trust me with your money."

A few months after we opened, Nashville sent a team to the Carter County House to learn more about what we were doing. They hoped to create some kind of continuing education for other caseworkers throughout Tennessee, and they wanted to interview a few of the caseworkers from our county.

About five caseworkers came to the Isaiah 117 House and sat around the dining room table answering questions. If the camera had focused on either me or Pam Harr as we sat to the side, it would have caught us with our mouths hanging open, marveling at the ripple effects created by one idea to better love foster children and that community.

I sat listening to caseworkers share about how they felt appreciated for the first time ever through the house. How they felt like they were able to breathe a little better knowing it was there. How they were able to make phone calls about finding placements for children in private, so that the child they were caring for didn't have to feel a sense of rejection if the family said no. How they were thankful for a cup of coffee, for kind words, for resources available to them.

A few weeks before that, one of the caseworkers sitting in the interview that day had been required to go to Memphis at the last minute, which is a nine-hour drive. She'd had to leave late that night and didn't have time to pack anything, so I'd said to her, "Well, I'm going to the Walmart to get things for the child. And I'm going to get things for you, too." She had tried to say she didn't need anything, but I insisted.

"Yes, I'm going to buy you some pajamas and underwear and other overnight necessities," I had told her. And if you don't tell me what size you wear, I'm going to get you size small so as not to offend. So if you're not a size small, you're going to need to tell me because either way I'm getting you something."

On the panel that day, she told that story and said into the camera, "Ronda made sure I had everything I needed. She bought me *underwear*." Her gratitude for something like that struck me. Who knows the blessings that can flow from one simple step of obedience?

THERE'S ALSO something called Children's Advocacy Day that happens in Nashville each year. That year, I was invited to speak. After saying yes, I found out that the time slot I was given was on the afternoon of the last day. Come to find out, basically everyone leaves at lunch on the last day, so I would be speaking to a mostly empty room—which was fine with me! Why were they letting me on stage at all at an event like this? I was just thankful to be a part of it.

On the first day of the conference, however, the man in charge came up to me and said, "Hey, listen, I know you're supposed to speak tomorrow afternoon, but we would love to move you to today. You'd go on at 10 a.m. between the Tennessee governor and the commissioner for child welfare." I looked at him, speechless for a second, and finally communicated to him that, yes, I would be okay with that change.

As I walked away, I marveled again at God's provision. I was a cheer and dance coach, and God had just picked me up out of the worst time slot and threw me on the main stage when everyone was right there to hear the governor of Tennessee. It's all His story; I just get to tell it.

And that's what I did. I stood on a state-sponsored stage that morning and talked about the goodness of God and how He had built a house for children He'd never forgotten. I told of how the house was miraculously provided and a few stories of children who had already been served by it.

Throughout the next two days following my talk, multiple caseworkers came up to me, all saying the same thing: "We have to have this in our community."

A news crew wanted to interview me, and they pulled me into a small room—basically a closet —to set everything up. As I sat there waiting for the interview to begin, I had a realization. Before speaking, I had been worried about how much of my faith I could bring into the talk. After all, it was a state event, and surely there were rules about that sort of thing.

But as I sat in that room with those TV producers or whoever they were, it felt as if God and I had found this secret loophole. I was telling *my* story about what has happened in *my* life. And what has happened in my life is that God has both inspired and accomplished everything to do with the Isaiah 117 House. I can stand on any stage and tell my story, and my story is God's story.

I laughed a little to myself as I praised God once again for making a way. As the camera started rolling, I resolved that I would never pass up an opportunity to give Him the glory.

A FEW MONTHS into getting the Carter County House off the ground and running successfully, someone brought up the idea for us to talk to a judge from Greene County, Tennessee, about potentially opening a second Isaiah 117 House in their area. Shortly after that, Joni and I found ourselves bringing a barbeque lunch to the juvenile court judge's office to meet him and get his initial thoughts.

From telling the story of Isaiah 117 House so many times, I've learned something. I get a lot of different reactions, but almost from the first few words I can see it in their eyes: If they're with me, they get it. Well, I sat in front of that judge whose job it is to remove children from their parents, and as soon as I started talking, I could tell he was with me. When I finished, he had tears in his eyes and told me, "Greene County needs this. Tell me what we do next."

That was the first time I'd ever thought through how the first house actually came together. The main thing I could think of was the importance of getting a board together to make it happen. So, a couple weeks later I met with the dozen or so new Greene County board members who'd been gathered by that judge.

For the next year, the judge had me speaking everywhere and anywhere that would have me. I spoke to every single church known to man within those county lines. One day, I pulled up to this little bitty Methodist church, and the sign outside said, "Let's build this house." Inside the church was one of those old-timey wooden signs on the wall saying the number of Bibles last week, number in attendance at Sunday School, and so on. The attendance the week before was seventy-two.

That church handed me a $7,000 check. They had been saving for that day, for that house. It was unbelievable and beautiful—I was watching a second community rally together! We were also given some land by a family in town, and we held a luncheon for others who might donate. Afterward, a contractor walked up to me and said, "I think I'm supposed to help you build this house."

He rallied some of his buddies, and I got invited to a meeting at a real estate office. Sitting in the conference room were three competing contractors who had already reviewed the house plans and written down everything that was needed. When I arrived, they were literally dividing up the responsibilities.

"I'll call Steve because he does all my plumbing."

"I can get Bill to do the drywall."

Those three competing contractors worked together to build a brand new home for $37,500 in one hundred days. I've said it before and I'll say it again:

Only. God.

After that house, we adopted a new term for our expansion plan called the "Loaves and Fishes" model. Just like the little boy in the gospels brought his small lunch for one to Jesus and He turned it into a feast for five thousand, we aim to bring what little we have to God in faith, and then give Him the space to do whatever He wants with it.

It's so strange to look back now and see how God has been preparing us for this journey for years. Hindsight allows us to see how He uses all of it to mold us and shape us into who we are today. Early in Corey's and my marriage, we were pretty naive about what it meant to be "fiscally responsible." We weren't reckless, we just didn't know what we were doing and weren't careful. The only thing I'd ever been taught to do was to tithe, so that was the one thing that Corey and I made sure to do once we got married.

Other than that, we made zero sound financial decisions. After we had Sophie, I decided to stay at home with her while she was still little. Corey and I hadn't necessarily planned for that. We didn't look at a budget to determine whether that decision was feasible. We just made the decision and expected it to work out.

One morning a few months later, I got a call from a collection agency. And that was how we found out that we were flat broke. After a lot of tears and a big come-to-Jesus moment, we got ourselves together and Corey went off to work.

After he left I felt like I could actually let loose, and I called my best friend in a panic. She came over, and on that day I was introduced to Dave Ramsey and the wonders of the envelope system. She and I wrote down every bill that we owed and every dollar we earned, and then I started calling almost every subscription service we paid for to cancel. Side note, if you're ever struggling to get out of your gym membership, just start crying. They'll be happy to see you go.

When the dust settled, we had $800 in medical bills. And we had $37 to our name.

I updated Corey when he came home from work, and he said, "I'm supposed to write our tithe check tomorrow."

"Write it," I responded.

The next day, we found a $350 insurance check from a few months ago that we'd never cashed. I called my dad, who was a banker, and asked if we were still allowed to deposit it. He said he was sure it'd be fine, and as we were getting off the phone, he said, "Ronda, do you need money?"

With a lump in my throat I responded, "Nope. We're good."

I deposited the check. The next day I went to speak at something that I thought I wasn't getting paid for, and they handed me a $500 check at the end. Within two days, $850 had come into our laps. And we never looked back. From then on and still to this day, we work hard to live below our means, and that financial philosophy has blessed us on multiple occasions!

Because of our personal experience with finances, I firmly believed in the importance of avoiding debt as we started the Isaiah 117 House. As I prayed about the logistics of our first house, the numbers that kept coming to my mind were $75,000 for the house and $75,000 to fully fund the first year's budget. That was our goal—to raise $150,000 and be debt-free before opening our doors.

You may be thinking, that's a crazy low amount of money. And you're right. But it's only crazy without God.

For every new house we build, we aim to raise $75,000 for the house and another $75,000 for our first year's budget. By all practical purposes, that's not nearly enough. But God makes it enough.

In Carter County, we bought a $140,000 house for $75,000, and then we got $90,000 worth of work done on it for free. With the same approach in Greene County, we brought our lunch of $75,000, and those three contractors built the house for $37,500.

Our third house is located in Washington County, Tennessee, and it got started through a mutual friend who connected me with a guy named Kelly Wolfe. That's all I knew about him —his name. I didn't even know what he did. But we met for lunch in Jonesborough, Tennessee, and I told him all about our mission and showed him our finances. After an hour-long conversation, we shook hands, said "nice to meet you," and went our separate ways.

Two weeks later he called me and said, "My wife and I have talked, and we want to buy you a house."

Another week passed, and he called again to tell me they had found a good option.

"It's $165,000, but it's got really good bones," he said. "It's definitely going to need some renovations, but if you'll pay the $65,000, we'll take care of the other $100,000."

We brought our $75,000, and God gave more than ten percent of that back to us.

That's the Loaves and Fishes model. To this day, God continues to take that little lunch we bring and multiply it, providing people, stirring up generosity, and creating a place for children to be loved.

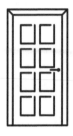

A Story from the House

WE HAD ALREADY HOSTED several younger kids, but one day we received the call for our first teenager. A fifteen-year-old was on her way to the house.

At the time, Sophie was fifteen, so you would've thought that I had this one in the bag. But actually, because I had Sophie I understood that there is no understanding a fifteen-year-old. So, those of us at the house were all a little concerned about what we were going to do. Obviously she wouldn't be like the younger kids; we couldn't blow bubbles or do anything we were used to.

Then, they called us back with more information. "By the way, she spent the night in juvenile detention because of a physical altercation with her mom." This did not make us feel any better.

We were working ourselves up into a frenzy, when I finally said (to myself as much as to the others), "Okay, we have got to focus. God built this house for anyone who walks through that door, and we are going to love everyone He brings. That's all we're going to do. We're going to love on whoever He brings."

We calmed down a little bit and got our bearings right as they opened the door. And what stood before me was not a big, mad, angry teenager. What stood before me was a small, scared, sad, broken little girl. And her head was down. Her hair was hiding her face. She was a redhead, just like my Isaiah.

I totally butchered the welcome because that's not what I was expecting. Finally, I kind of blurted out the words, "Would you like a shower?"

She peeked up at me and said, "I would love a shower." So Ms. Jody took her upstairs and laid out everything she needed.

Eventually, she came back down in some flannel pajamas with her hair in a messy bun, and Ms. Jody asked her, "Are you hungry?" She gave a little sound of assent and Ms. Jody responded, "Well, I'm going to fix you something to eat. I bet you haven't eaten anything good today."

We all gathered around the table and ate a meal together. When we were done, she started to open up and cry. She poured her heart out to us, releasing some of the stress and pain that had been building in her.

The caseworker who was there that night later told us, "That's not something that we see happen in an office. That happens when someone gets a shower, gets a meal, and feels safe. That happens in a home."

Chapter Nine

E ach new house that popped up was a surprise and a blessing. Isaiah 117 House was growing, slowly but surely. For me, any growth at all was beyond what I had dreamed. But God had even more in mind.

In the fall of 2019, my husband and I were contacted by a woman named Lea, who emailed us something along the lines of, "I'm part of a small documentary company. We are currently traveling the country doing a story from every state. We haven't done one in Tennessee yet, and we haven't done one about foster care, but we heard about you and think it would be cool to interview you about Isaiah 117

House. Here's the link to our website; let me know if you're interested."

That's all I knew. I went to the website, which didn't look super up-to-date, and honestly, I was skeptical. I wouldn't have been surprised at that point if it had been a scam. But, I try to be open to anything that comes my way, because who knows what could lead to something? Trying my best to live a life of obedience and say yes! So, I called her back and told her I'd love to learn more.

We scheduled a call, during which I explained again the story of the house. I heard the same phrase again: "We're a small documentary company." And still, that was basically all that I knew. She had seen a video of me talking about foster care in Tennessee on, ironically, the one thing I had fought against in the beginning: the Facebook. A few days later, Lea reached out after taking it to her committee to let us know that we had been selected for the Tennessee story.

Before it became official, I had to sign some kind of document. I'll admit that I thought something weird was going on, and I sent the papers to my lawyer asking for his thoughts. He read it and said it seemed completely harmless, adding, "If they show up the day of and all of a sudden they want money or anything, just say no." That sounded simple enough, so I signed it, sent it back, and it was official—a small documentary company was coming to film a story on Isaiah 117 House.

Before they came to film, however, we were going to have one more visitor. A girl by the name of Sarah was going to come for a meeting in January. I was told the meeting could be anywhere, so my new friend Sarah from the possibly sketchy documentary company came and sat on my couch to meet me in person and hear my story.

That week, Isaiah had just had his tonsils out, so I wasn't thinking much about anything besides taking care of him. So, Sarah came and sat on my couch while Isaiah lay on a beanbag across the room, recovering. Let's just say she got a very real version of us.

As Sarah was leaving, she told me the crew would be there later that week to film for two days. That was all well and good, and Sarah seemed normal and nice. My lawyer said I hadn't signed over my money to them, and it would hopefully get the word out to more people about our ministry.

But then, Isaiah became severely dehydrated, something that a lot of kids do when they get their tonsils out. However, he also started showing symptoms for a rare and serious virus.

On the day before the film crew came, Corey and I rushed Isaiah to the children's hospital in town. I wasn't spending a single second thinking about making time for that film crew anymore. My child was in the hospital—how could I care about anything else?

At that point, this "small documentary company" did something they had never done before. They looped the spouse into the big surprise that they had been planning all along. While I was in the hospital, Corey received a phone call letting him know that Mike Rowe was currently flying into Tennessee and that Isaiah 117 House was going to be featured on his show, *Returning the Favor*, a popular Facebook video series with extensive viewership and engagement.

Apparently, they normally didn't like telling anyone close to the situation what was really going on because usually that meant the surprise was spoiled before it could actually be revealed. But, this was a special situation because, heaven knows, I wasn't planning to budge from Isaiah's side without some encouragement from my close people.

That evening, I was lying in the hospital bed with Isaiah as Corey sat in the chair right next to us. Then, out of nowhere, he said, "Hey, I was just thinking that if Isaiah is still in the hospital tomorrow, I can just stay with him so that you can go do that documentary thing."

I sat up and looked at him as if he suddenly had five heads. "Are you crazy?" I should have known something was up at that point because ordinarily he wouldn't have suggested something like that, but I just laid back down, which left Corey to deal with the outcome that he had predicted.

He called them back to let them know. "She ain't coming. I don't know what else to tell you. Don't plan on her being there tomorrow." They were at such a loss at what to do, I think they were about to tell me the truth.

The hospital had been giving Isaiah fluids and everything he needed, and right about that time, he started to perk up. Pretty soon, he was running up and down the halls, and it became clear that nothing was wrong with him besides being dehydrated. After a long and stressful day, we were cleared to go home.

The next morning, I woke up feeling like I'd been hit by a truck. And then I received another sign that something different was going on. My friend Christy called me that morning and said, "Don't you have that documentary thing today? Do you want me to bring you coffee and drive you to the Isaiah House for the filming?"

Again, I was so tired that this sign got past me, too. I accepted, and a few minutes later she stood next to me in my bathroom as I got ready. I didn't care a bit about what I looked like. *It's just a small documentary thing*, I thought. I didn't fix my hair or choose my outfit carefully. I did, however, take the time to put my fake lashes on. There I was, in my finest hour, wishing I was still asleep but instead standing at my bathroom counter and trying not to cry while I glued on my fake lashes.

We finally arrived at the Carter County house, and I saw a lot of Isaiah 117 House people standing around. That didn't tip me off, either, because it made sense that the crew would want to interview families and volunteers and case-workers. If you ever get to watch our episode on Mike Rowe's Facebook page, just know that my shocked reaction is genuine.

I gathered everyone inside and got their attention. And, please keep in mind that every single person there knew what was actually going on except for me.

"Here's the deal," I said. "This is a small documentary company coming in a few minutes, and you all know I don't do details, so I have no idea what's about to happen. But there are two rules, so listen up. Rule number one: Do not say anything negative about the Department of Children's Services. I don't care what your experience has been; you're not going to be filmed saying anything negative about them."

They were all nodding their heads at me, and I continued. "Rule number two: Nobody takes their clothes off during this interview process. I'm telling you right now, I've seen their website and it looks a little sketch. If anyone asks you to take your shirt off, it's not that kind of video. I don't know these people, so just be careful."

That was literally the pep talk I gave. Right after I finished speaking, there was a knock at the door and then a camera crew rushed in with lights and boom mics. Some guy I'd never met came over to me, pulled my shirt out, and dropped a mic down. I looked around at everybody, trying to communicate to them, "See, that's what I'm talking about. He's already in my shirt. I'm telling you, be on guard. This could be totally sketch."

I sat at the kitchen table, still not grasping any concept of what was going on, and watching the chaos around me. Then, the front door opened again and a man walked in. Judging by everyone else's reaction in the room, I was supposed to know who this guy was.

He walked over to me and said, "Hey, I'm Mike. Nice to meet you, Ronda." All I could do was smile and nod and hope that I'd have a chance to ask someone without a camera in their face what in the world was happening.

Finally, I pulled Christy aside and whispered, "Is that the guy from that show *Tim the Tool Man Taylor?*"

"First of all, that's not what the TV show is called," she whispered back. "Second, we're mic'd right now, so everyone can still hear what you're saying."

So much for being polite about it.

Throughout the day, I slowly put more pieces together. I eventually learned what Mike Rowe did, but from first shaking his hand I already knew that he was kind, real, and funny. He had a way of putting everybody around him at ease.

About mid-morning, Mike approached me and told me we were going on a trip to the Department of Children's Services. I guess I still didn't have everything figured out, because my first thought was of the lady in charge over there at the time, Sherri Lawson. I kept thinking to myself, *They're not going to let us in. Sherri's going to kill me. She will kill me if I bring a camera crew into her office!* But what was I supposed to do—Mike Rowe was with me! As we pulled up, there stood Sherri Lawson, waving to us. Finally, it clicked that this had been the plan for everybody except me for a long time.

I had never seen *Returning the Favor* before, so I didn't know I should be expecting a surprise at the end. Our final stop of the day was to what I believed was a family photo shoot. On my way there with my new friend Mike, I found out that the secretary for the Washington County, Tennessee, Department of Children's Services office knew about the show and had nominated me eight times.

Mike told me they had never had anyone nominated that many times before. Earlier that day, Mike had even taken flowers to her house to meet her. Now, as we pulled up once again to the Isaiah 117 Resource Center, I saw her standing there, ready to greet us.

Mike escorted me around the side of the house, and I then experienced one of the biggest surprises of my life. Waiting for me there was a host of people I cared for, and who cared for me and for Isaiah 117 House. The Milligan University cheerleaders and dancers I had coached, foster parents, contractors we had worked with, and my family were just a few of the groups of

people I saw in the backyard. It was unbe-
lievable.

MIKE ROWE and his amazing team visited the
Carter County Isaiah 117 House in January
2020. However, the episode wasn't set to air
until March 16.

Joy and I had made plans to publicize the airing
of the episode. She had planned a social media
blitz, watch parties in different communities, the
works. But then, on Sunday night, March 8,
Sarah from Mike's team called me.

"Hey, there's been a change of plans," she said.
"Your episode is being moved to tomorrow."

Our publicity plans went out the window, so we
just did what we could to get the word out
within one day. On Monday night, my family
and I gathered around the TV to watch. I had
been nervous that they would get something
wrong in telling our story—after all, they had
only been with us for a few hours and had to fit
everything into a 24-minute episode. But I
shouldn't have worried. They told our story so

well. Nothing was misrepresented; nothing was painted in a negative light.

My only disappointment was that I'd been thinking we could show the video in churches I visited. But unfortunately, I cussed in the middle of the episode, and they had to bleep it. No good for showing in sanctuaries. *But if that's my only complaint*, I thought, *I'll take it.*

The next day, our phones start ringing. By March 11, we'd gotten a map of the United States so we could color in the states where the calls were coming from. People were wanting to start their own Isaiah 117 Houses. By March 12, almost the entire map was colored in. At the time, Isaiah 117 House only employed four people, and we didn't have a plan—not a single document—on how to get houses in so many new places.

That Friday, I had a meeting with a judge and a caseworker. While there, the caseworker said, "If it's okay, I have to take a selfie with you. My wife loves Mike Rowe, and we watched your episode on Monday." We laughed and took the picture. Later, I learned that two million people watched the Isaiah 117 House episode on March 9.

On March 13, 2020, the world shut down. By March 16, the day our episode was originally supposed to air, all eyes were glued to news stations as a global pandemic made its way into our backyard. Instead of watching Returning the Favor, people were panicking about school closures, going to work, and getting paid. The episode that aired on March 16th only had 10,000 viewers. It felt like God literally picked us up and moved us up one week. Two million people watched, and for that reason, around the office, we still talk about the growth of the nonprofit as "Pre-Mike Rowe" and "Post-Mike Rowe."

When the world shut down, we four employees got to work. We had a new goal: to reverse-engineer everything we had done up to that point. We had to have a thorough understanding of how we worked and an organized strategy for growth in order to keep up with the new demand.

One idea we had was to have anyone wanting to start an Isaiah 117 House in their community submit a video to us. That way, we could more easily vet the interested groups. Ever since we first implemented that requirement in March

2020, we have received at least one video per week.

I'll never forget talking on the phone with a woman from California who wanted to start a house in her community. During our conversation in 2020, she asked me how many children were in the custody of the state of Tennessee.

"Eight thousand," I said.

"Ronda," she responded, "There are eight thousand children in the custody of the state in my *county*."

I got off the phone with the same feeling I'd had way back in the DCS conference room in 2014. The problem was too big. There were so many children affected by foster care at that very moment. It was impossible to help them all. Everything we did felt so small and insignificant. *God*, I prayed silently, *You've got the wrong girl. I'm in over my head.*

All of a sudden, in my mind I saw an image of myself standing in front of a big pool of water holding a little bitty rock. And God kept telling me, "Drop the rock, Ronda. Just let go and drop the rock." I let go of that little bitty rock and watched as it hit the water and sent ripples out across the still surface.

"You just drop the rock." I heard God say, "And I'll take care of the ripples."

So, I got up and kept moving forward, and I've watched in awe as the ripples have simply kept on going.

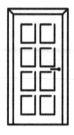

A Story from the House

IT WAS a hot August day on the first day of school. I got a call that three girls would be coming to the house. They were of preschool, elementary, and high school ages, and they had all just watched their dad kill their mom's boyfriend.

I was already at the house, and I notified the volunteers who were on call that I would stay with the girls until someone else could come. When the three girls arrived, we all ended up in the backyard. The littlest one was swinging, and she seemed to be very unaware of what had happened. It was surreal to see her laughing and playing as if her little eyes hadn't just witnessed a horrific event.

The high schooler was mad. "I cannot believe he did this," she kept saying. "This was the first day of school. I was supposed to see my friends today."

The elementary-aged girl sat to the side in their case-worker's lap, crying. She couldn't stop, and through her tears she said, "I really wanted to meet my teacher today."

About that time, the volunteer on call came around the corner into the backyard. I looked up from my place next to the swing and saw Debbie Estep. I didn't think much of it until I heard Debbie call this little girl by name. Then, my jaw dropped.

"Oh my goodness," Debbie said, "We missed you at school today."

It was her teacher.

The little girl jumped down and ran to Debbie and gave her a tight hug. Debbie hugged her right back, and they spent the rest of the day together. On that day, likely one of the most traumatic of her life, that little girl experienced love. She experienced warmth. She experienced tangible evidence that even in her heartache, she was not alone.

Things like this don't just happen again and again without an explanation. The fact that her teacher was the volunteer on call that afternoon is nothing short of specific provision from God Himself.

And it keeps happening.

We've had kids show up to the house with a few big boxes and say, "I used my birthday money to buy Barbies because I just kept thinking, 'If I was away from my mom, I would want Barbies.'" We'd get a picture and thank them.

An hour later, we'd get a call about another placement, and a girl would walk in and say, "Oh, Barbies! That's my favorite."

God is so real. He's real and He's active; He's orchestrating, and He's redeeming. I can't explain abuse, and I can't explain why there even has to be an Isaiah 117 House. But I can know that God is right there with His children. And when I forget it, I learn it all over again the next time I see Him at work.

I pray that even if the little girl with her arms wrapped around her teacher's waist didn't understand it then, somewhere in her heart the truth became more real to her. Little one, you are not alone.

Chapter Ten

I've talked a lot so far about everything God was doing in bringing about the Isaiah 117 House ministry during those years. But another obvious and important angle to consider is the one within the context of my own family—where our journey with foster care began!

When Isaiah came to us, it quickly became apparent that there were some aspects of foster care for which we had not been prepared. For example, when a family accepts a foster placement, the parents must get them to a health department to see a doctor within the first two or three days. I knew that. What I didn't know was Isaiah's full name. Or his Social Security number. Or anything about his medical history.

I loaded up this baby who I'd known for twelve hours, and we rolled up to our 8 a.m. appointment at the health department, oblivious about what we were getting into.

When I went to check him in, I was of course asked all of those questions and had to keep saying, "I don't know." I became increasingly discouraged. Here I was, the one entrusted with caring for this precious child, and I didn't even know him. Thankfully, they had a system and were able to find his information, but it was heartbreaking to see his vulnerability manifested in yet another way.

It also didn't help that the woman behind the counter became increasingly cold and impatient with me. I stood in front of her with my Vera Bradley tote bag and brand-new stroller, and I didn't know the answers to her questions or understand her lingo. She was not impressed.

It felt like I'd been transported into another world that I was expected to automatically understand and operate within. It was a world of acronyms, implied expectations, and common sense that could only be known by having lived the same situation before. It was overwhelming.

But, those who know me often hear me say, "Shoulders back, chin up, here I go." As I was in my car crying because I felt like a failure, I also sensed that I had been built for this. I sat forward and said to myself, "Shoulders back, chin up, here I go." I had a kid with me who needed me and, apparently, I had no one to help me. From that point on, I was determined to be strong and to do whatever it took to get this baby, whom I already loved so much, everything he could possibly need.

A few days later, I got a call that we needed to schedule a CFTM. Still not over the health department visit, I was too embarrassed to ask what that meant. Corey had something at the same time, and we both agreed that it would be fine if he didn't go. Surely it couldn't be that big of a deal, right?

I walked into the DCS office for the CFTM, and they directed me to a conference room. I sat down at the table across from a couple who, come to find out, were Isaiah's birth parents. I learned that day that CFTM stands for Child and Family Team Meeting, and that this was to be the first CFTM of many. I met Isaiah's birth parents for the first time, alone and unprepared.

The room was tense. The parents saw me as an opponent and were very defensive. And you know, I get it. They had lost their child over the weekend, and I was the one who had him. The first five minutes were dedicated to Isaiah. The caseworker asked me a generic question on how he was doing, and I fumbled out an answer. Then for the next fifty-five minutes, I learned about the lives of Isaiah's parents. They were working with the caseworker to lay out their permanency plan—if they were to ever get Isaiah back, they would need to fulfill certain requirements to show they were capable of caring for him—so I listened as they talked through everything that would need to change.

And honestly, as someone who has lived a privileged life, the things they were being asked to do sounded really easy. Things like: get a stable job, have housing, attend a drug recovery program —that had to be pretty doable, right? I left that meeting and, in my ignorance, I believed Isaiah would be back with his parents within six weeks.

But something that looks easy to accomplish to someone like me, who grew up in a loving home, who has never been afraid at night or worried where the next meal would come from, looks very different to someone who has not had those experiences. It turned out that a list that seemed doable to me was virtually impossible to someone with different life experiences.

That was my first Child and Family Team Meeting. What I noticed over the next few years during those visits planted a seed for Isaiah 117 House, because it was the same every time: five minutes for the child, fifty-five minutes for the parents. That concerned me. Shouldn't there be more time, energy, and resources spent on the well-being of the child whose life was being affected by the poor decisions others were making? If a child has been removed from their home because it's believed that they are in imminent danger of death or harm, then the focus needs to be on what is best for the child going forward.

Over the next two years, I interacted with Isaiah's biological parents a lot. I saw Isaiah's biological mom almost every Friday for her visitation time with him. She wasn't able to do anything else on her permanency plan, but she took advantage of almost every opportunity to see him.

So, every Friday morning at 10:00, I would sit in the lobby with Isaiah and wait for her to come in. Then, I would hand Isaiah to her and watch as they walked into an adjoining room and shut the door behind them for the next two hours.

Later, I was able to process how difficult those days truly were. For every other hour of the week, you, the foster parent, are in charge of that child. His eating, sleeping, safety, happiness. You are his comforter when he cries. You know his likes and dislikes. But every Friday morning at 10:00, you're reminded that in spite of that, he is not your child, and that even though you love him with your whole heart and believe he's safer with you, there is a strong chance that he will go back to his biological family.

Each week, his mom would open the door after two hours had passed and hand Isaiah back to me. We'd drive away, and she'd be left standing outside the Department of Children's Services, smoking a cigarette and devastated because she'd handed her child back to me.

I was devastated by the brokenness of all of it—me trying to detach Isaiah from my arms as he cried for me, having such a raw moment happen in the middle of a lobby while people sat and watched, watching a mother grieve that her child was not fully hers while also feeling my own grief that he was not fully mine. It was shocking, and the pain felt fresh each time.

I attended every court hearing involving Isaiah's parents. I sat in the room, listening to them lie. The lies weren't malicious; they just wanted their son back. And as a foster parent, I had no authority to stand up and say they were lying. I just had to sit still and pray—pray that the truth would be seen, and that God's will would be done. I'd pray that if the truth was that Isaiah needed to go back to his parents, that God would let me see the truth. And if the truth was that Isaiah wouldn't be safe back in that home, that He would let the judge see that.

During that period of time, I arrived at a difficult conclusion. The ultimate goal of the child welfare system is to reunite the child with his parents, but sometimes the system pursues that goal to a fault. In this world, reunification is not always the best answer. That's a hard thing to admit, and it's not a popular opinion. But it's what I've lived.

At the same time I hold to that conviction, I also don't doubt for a second that Isaiah's parents love him. What I explain to Isaiah every chance I get is that he was and always will be one loved little boy. He was born to his biological parents, and they love him. Corey and I get to raise him, and we love him. It's illness that keeps his biological parents from him—drugs, alcohol, toxic relationships. Those things are hard to shake, and even though they wanted to, they just couldn't do it. In such a broken world, the question is so much bigger than whether or not the parents love their child.

It's easy to pass judgment on the parents who can't keep up with the permanency plan, to say, "If you actually loved your kid, you wouldn't choose an abusive husband. If you loved your kid, you would stop doing drugs." But if the love from an abusive husband is all you've ever known, or if drugs are the only thing that has made you feel good since you were twelve, it's hard to simply walk away from that.

As the court hearings were going on and the Friday morning visits continued, I got to know the parents a little better. I was also stalking their Facebook pages like it was my job. (By the way, that's not a healthy course of action.) Over time, I understood more of the reasons why their lives looked the way they did.

There were some serious red flags around sending a little boy home with them. I became more and more of a defender for Isaiah. If the parents want their child back no matter what, and the state wants the reunification of families above all else, who looks out for the best interests of the child in question?

A foster parent frequently becomes an advocate for the child they're fostering. The thing is, you can't halfway love a baby. You can only love a baby one hundred percent. So when you say yes to a foster child, you love that child. And if it's best for the child to go back to his family, you love him one hundred percent and you give the child back. But if the child shouldn't go back, you become a fierce fighter on his behalf, and you love him one hundred percent as you fight for his safety.

One night in the midst of this battle, Corey, Sophie, Mac, and I were sitting together watching *Animal Planet*. There was a special on what happens when a baby animal loses its mom and is left in the wild. The episode showed other species coming to take the baby in—and they were crazy stories!

One example was a greyhound dog that started raising a baby deer in the backyard of a woman's house. They would nap, play, and eat together, and eventually the deer grew up and left. But every now and then, that deer would come back and visit its greyhound mom.

There was a story of a cat raising baby ducks. And there were even stories of nurturing relationships formed between animals who were classified as predator and prey. Somehow, the mommas knew to care for the babies.

Sitting on our couch with my family all asleep around me (I guess no one else cared), I exclaimed, "See, even the wild animals get it!" That woke everybody up, and they all stared at me as if to say, "Oh my gosh, she's finally lost it."

I was too excited to care. It so perfectly illustrated the point that every baby needs a momma, and that God would provide a stand-in when one was needed. For the next year, I brought up that *Animal Planet* special to anyone who would listen. To everyone I talked to, I ended up asking a variation of the question, "Did you see the special on *Animal Planet*?" My kids would roll their eyes and say, "No, Mom. No one saw that special except for you."

So often, when I talk about foster care, people respond by saying they could never do what we do. They couldn't stand the thought of taking in a child because of the risk of heartbreak if they had to give them up. They couldn't commit to taking in a child because of the unknown impact that it would have on their family. But what hit so close to home with me about watching a cat care for baby ducks is that, ultimately, it's not about us. There is a child that needs a parent and, look, even a cat knows its responsibility.

When we hear a call to take in a child, we can't factor in the likelihood that some aspect of saying yes would be inconvenient to us. Of course it's inconvenient, but it's about the child. Maybe they need a home for six months, maybe two years, or maybe the rest of their life. It's not up to us to know the answer to that. As with anything God calls us to, all we have to do is say yes.

IN THE SUMMER OF 2017, the day finally came when the court was to decide if Isaiah's mom's rights would be terminated. I gave my testimony and then had to immediately get on a plane and fly to New York for a friend's funeral. So, it was just a little bit of an emotionally charged day.

As I sat on the plane waiting for takeoff, I got a message from the caseworker. "It's not looking good." Before I could get any more context behind that heart-wrenching text, the plane began to taxi. Phones off.

With that message running circles in my mind, I put my head in my hands, and time stood still. I was praying so hard that I didn't even know we had touched down in New York until I felt someone touch my shoulder. It was a stewardess; the entire plane was already empty.

I got off the plane and turned my phone back on, looking feverishly for a text update. Finally, I gave up and called the caseworker. She answered and immediately just said, "We got him. We got him."

Right there in the airport I dropped to my knees, crying. I'd had only one thought that went through my head as I waited for our case-worker to pick up: *If we lose him, how will I tell Sophie? He's her brother. How am I supposed to tell her that he won't be with us anymore?*

Fostering a child is the hardest thing I've ever done. But it is right to take up the cause of the fatherless and defend the oppressed. And for those two little boys who God brought to our family, I'd do it again and again and again.

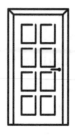

A Story from the House

WE GOT a call that "a sixteen-year-old male with anger issues" was on his way to the house. We normally get notified a few hours before the caseworker and child arrive, but on this day, I was still on the phone with the caseworker when she said, "Oh my word, they're pulling into the driveway right now."

We hung up as they walked in the door. He was incredibly polite, and he seemed to be calm and kind. "I'm happy to turn something on the TV for you if you want," I said.

He sat down on the couch and said, "That'd be great."

I tried to get the TV turned on, but I kept having technical difficulties, which is the story of my life. Finally, I looked at the TV and said, "Oh, Spectrum, you are making me so mad."

With my back to him, I said, "Do you ever get mad?"

Then, I heard in a small, cracked voice, "That's kind of how I ended up here." I turned around in time to see a big tear roll down his cheek.

Later that day, I called the caseworker to get more information on this sweet boy with anger issues. She told me that his dad was in prison. His mom had died of an overdose that summer, and he had been the one to find her. After she passed, he went to live with an uncle in government housing.

One night, he got mad and threw a chair out of a window. Long story short, he was in state custody because he had nowhere else to go. And because of the label on his file—"sixteen-year-old with anger issues"—no one wanted to take him in. His caseworkers had to turn to their only other option, which was to send him to a detention center in Memphis.

I called the house to check in, and the volunteer told me, "He's really scared, Ronda. He's crying. They're telling him he has to go to Memphis." I told her to ask him what he needed. We hung up, and a few minutes later she texted me two words: "wave cap."

Now, I had no earthly idea what a wave cap might be, but I was already en route to the Walmart and deter-

mined to find one. I was still just as confused when I got inside, so I called a former student of mine who could help me . . .

I stood in the middle of the Walmart, having this conversation on speakerphone because my cell wasn't working properly at the time. I gave her the rundown and finally got to my reason for calling her.

"You don't know what a wave cap is?" she responded.

"Okay, this is no time for judgment. Just help me."

She laughed at me, then directed me toward the one shelf in the store that might have what we needed. She asked if I saw anything that might look right, and I answered, "Um, I see a lime green wrap."

She immediately shut that down. "Ronda, no. Hold on. I'm going to hang up and text you a picture of what it should look like."

We hung up, and I started to leave the aisle to get some other things while I waited for the picture. As I was walking away, a woman standing nearby stopped me and said, "Are you Mrs. Paulson?"

I stopped and looked at her, and I realized that it was a girl I had taught at the high school in Elizabethton years before. We caught up a little, and I told her what I was looking for and asked her to pray for me to find one.

A few minutes later, when I was on the other side of the store, I heard over the loudspeaker: "Ronda Paulson to pharmacy. Ronda Paulson to pharmacy."

I started speed walking in that direction because I knew what was waiting for me. As I rounded the corner, there stood my ex-student, jumping up and down and waving a wave cap in the air.

As I drove home, I thought to myself, I don't know if this is going to make any sense to him, but I have to tell him this story. He was sitting on the living room couch when I walked in, and I pulled up the ottoman to sit in front of him. "Can I tell you a crazy story?" I asked.

He said yes, and I walked him through everything that had happened. Then I looked him in the eye and said, "Do you get it? Do you get what I'm saying? God has never left you, and He's never going to leave you. He's already in Memphis, and He was in the Walmart, and He was with you when you found your mom. And He's never leaving you. He is always going before you, and He loves you. He loves you. And God wanted you to have this wave cap."

He responded, "Will you pray with me?"

And we prayed over that boy.

I don't know where he is today. But that night we prayed over him and had revival in the middle of that Isaiah 117 House—over a wave cap.

Chapter Eleven

A nother important piece to the Isaiah 117 House ministry is the final addition to our family: Eli. In the fall of 2016, before I'd ever called the first board meeting for Isaiah 117 House, we found out that Isaiah's mom was pregnant again.

During one of our visits with our caseworker, she asked me, "If the baby is removed, would you be willing to take him in? In the event that the new baby enters into the state's custody, we always reach out to the foster parents that have the sibling first."

I didn't answer her question right away, but I asked what she meant. She continued, "Well, the baby will go home with his mom first."

"Wait, what?" I asked.

"Yeah. Every mom gets a chance to mother."

"But," I said, "You took Isaiah from her because he wasn't safe."

"Yes, but this is a new baby, so it's considered a new case."

I couldn't believe what I was hearing. It was a new baby, but the same parents. How could it be considered a new case if it was the same parents with the same struggles? Every time I followed up on that question, I got the same answer: In the eyes of the law, every mother gets a chance to mother. Judges, caseworkers, and child advocates all answered the same.

It was as if that had been the accepted answer for so long that no one questioned it anymore. It reminded me of those Febreze commercials where the person is nose-blind to the bad smell after having been in it for so long. But entering the system as an outsider, this didn't sit right with me at all. How could a new baby magically be safe with people who hadn't shown any signs of being fit parents for the child they already had?

As it got closer to time for Eli to be born, Corey and I sat down to talk everything through. We had both come home for lunch, and it was just the two of us. While we were eating, I got a call from the caseworker. By the time we hung up, I was crying, and Corey asked what was wrong.

"There's a baby coming," I told him.

"I know."

"And they keep asking if we will take the baby."

"I know."

"And I don't feel like we can say yes."

"Why not?"

"Well, because I begged for Sophie and I begged for Mac, and then I basically tricked you into fostering Isaiah. Surely there's a limit to your goodness. I feel like I've pushed the envelope."

"You're seriously crying because you think I would say no?" He asked.

"Won't you?"

He looked straight at me and said, "Ronda, we are taking that baby!"

And then I was really crying—at the goodness of my husband, at the goodness of God to give me my husband, and at the possibility of being a safe place for this new little life.

A few weeks later, on March 6, 2017, Eli was born. We had made the decision that if Eli were removed, we would say yes. The way my friend, Christy, describes me during the time between March 6 and March 30, when he came to us, was that I just paced. My child was out there somewhere, not safe, and I had to get to him. I called the caseworkers every day. I called the child advocates. I called the hotline. I fussed with Darlene at the DCS receptionist desk. I did everything in the world I could think of to get it across that this baby was not safe.

A five-pound baby boy lived with parents who had done nothing to change anything that they had been asked to change. The mom wasn't allowed alone with Isaiah; the dad wasn't allowed anywhere near him because he had failed so many drug tests. But those same people were allowed to take home an infant. I'd say to anyone who would listen, "What's more defenseless than a five-pound baby? He can't run. He can't feed himself. There is no way that he's okay."

For three weeks I was a complete wreck. Then, I finally got the call I'd been waiting for. Eli was being removed and would be brought to our house later that night.

"Later that night" ended up being 11 p.m. because there had been a situation. Earlier in the day, the parents had gotten into a fight that ended with the dad throwing a couch through a window. Glass shattered with a five-pound baby boy lying right there. The mom called the police, and they showed up to a trailer in shambles. When they arrived, she tried to lie and take it all back, and they ended up offering her a deal. If she would sign a piece of paper saying that she would not see Isaiah and Eli's father anymore, she could keep Eli. Again, the fact that she was even offered another chance blows my mind, but praise the Lord, she wouldn't sign it.

When Eli arrived at our house, he reeked of cigarette smoke. His mom had sent one dirty bottle with him; she didn't want to provide anything to help us care for him because she was so mad he was taken. Eli would not open his eyes. He would not cry. He would not eat. The next day I realized something was wrong with his mouth.

We were already planning to go to the health department, and by this time I was an old pro. (When they asked his name, I gave it in full confidence!) It turned out that he had thrush, and it was so bad on his cheeks, gums, and throat that he hadn't been eating.

With medicine and careful treatment, he began eating, and finally, at almost a month old, he started gaining weight. But, Eli did not open his eyes for about a month after he came to us. And he did not cry for almost two. I was told he had likely shut down from the trauma he had endured, which absolutely infuriated me. He should have never gone home with them.

Even after Eli finally came to us, my mind often went to what could have been. What if Eli had been on or near that couch the night his dad threw it? And, why in the world were we okay with waiting around for the parents to mess up before stepping in to help the baby? I repeatedly heard phrases like: "When we need to remove the baby . . ." and "When the parents mess up." It was so normal for those in the foster-care system to just assume that the biological parents wouldn't be able to raise their child, but to me it felt like we were running some type of experiment. With a baby.

I couldn't shake these concerns, and when I asked other people about it they would often respond, "Well, surely situations like Eli's don't always happen." But then it happened to a really good friend of mine. It was almost the exact same story. They brought a nine-month-old little boy home and about a year later his mom gave birth to another baby boy. She was moving from place to place and she was using, and he wasn't safe, but she got to take him with her anyway.

That caught my attention. What are the chances that this happened not only to us but also to another friend? And then it happened to yet another friend. All of a sudden, the same situation had happened three times within my little foster-care community.

With the encouragement from some of those friends, I reached out to Senator Jon Lundberg, who had been both a supporter and volunteer at Isaiah 117 House for years. I told him my dreams for something called Eli's Law. He helped us through the whole process, working on the language in the law and getting me to testify on the Senate floor about Eli and what he had experienced. And we got it passed!

Eli got to sit on the governor's lap as he signed Eli's Law. It was amazing to see Eli there, happy and healthy, knowing that they were signing something into legislation that would protect other little ones just like him so that they, too, could be happy and healthy.

Eli's Law, which is currently only in the state of Tennessee, states that if you currently have a child in custody, then a judge should look at the permanency plan and evaluate the amount of progress that's been made. If the parents found housing and jobs and have been doing their drug rehab—if they can prove that they can care for their new baby—by all means, they should be allowed to take the baby home. But, as in Eli's case, if they have not made progress in these areas, and if they can't prove their ability to care for a new baby, that baby should not be allowed to go home with them.

Eli's Law was signed into effect on June 25, 2021. On that day, the system in Tennessee shifted just a little bit more toward prioritizing the children. It had always been about giving the parents every possible chance. But since that day, it has become more about giving the child the ultimate chance—the chance to be safe, healthy, and loved in an environment that has proven it can provide those things.

ISAIAH AND ELI were both adopted into the Paulson family on the same day: November 17, 2018. There's a "117" in the middle of that date, which just feels like the cherry on top of a day that already felt so orchestrated by God.

It was a day of incredible joy and excitement. It was final! No more stressing about the what-ifs; no more visits or keeping up with the many rules that came with foster care. It was so exciting to be free of that and to finally change their last names to ours.

But there was also a sadness that came with the day. Adoption is beautiful, but it comes out of something broken. On a day that was so happy for us, there was also a momma who was grieving. For her, that day meant letting go of her dream of getting to be a family. I couldn't help but think of their mom even as we rejoiced, because I know that she loved them very much. The day held an interesting tension of mourning and joy. Adoption does not erase the brokenness, but it does offer redemption, and an invitation into a life of abundance and hope.

The day itself couldn't have been more beautiful. It was National Adoption Day, and family and friends gathered at the courthouse for a celebration. Later that night, we hosted a huge dance party and, at the boys' request, ate cupcakes and pizza. The theme was bowties, and I'd sent out invitations that looked like birth announcements that said "It's a Boy!" We had a picture frame there for guests to sign, and so many wrote how moved they were to see God's hand throughout the whole journey.

It was a blessing to me to see how many people were moved by what God had so clearly done. I truly believe that Isaiah and Eli didn't become

Paulsons because someone messed up. Their mom was supposed to have them, and we were supposed to raise them. This was meant to be their story all along. It's beautiful and heart-breaking; it's beauty from ashes. That's adoption, and desire for redemption is the heart behind Isaiah 117 House. To God be the glory.

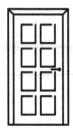

A Story from the House

IT'S NOT AN UNCOMMON SCENARIO. *A five-year-old little girl goes to kindergarten, spends the whole day just like her classmates, and as she's getting ready to leave is stopped in the hall by her principal, school counselor, and a woman she's never met. They tell her that she will not be allowed to get on the bus and that she will not be going home that day.*

That child is then taken to the principal's office, which is where you go when you're in trouble, and then eventually to a state office to wait. But, thankfully for some children who have days like these, there's an Isaiah 117 House in the community.

One little girl had this experience, and after school she was whisked away to be lavishly loved on by two volunteers: Ms. Corey and Ms. Jody. They went all out in making this little girl feel special. They got her food. They got her a bath. They found out there was a program at school the next day, and they gave her a new dress and a matching bow. Later that night, a foster placement was found, and they gathered everything that the foster placement needed and then sent her off to the next portion of her foster care journey. And that's normally where our part of the story ends. But this particular story happened in a small town.

A few months later, the foster parents reached out and said that she was getting ready to turn six. "We told her the sky's the limit," they said. "It's whatever she wants. Chuck E. Cheese, a trampoline park, renting out the community pool—we were ready for anything she might want to do on her birthday. But when we asked her, she just said that 'she wanted to go back to the Isaiah 117 House that is the most fun house ever.' And she also requested that her best friends Ms. Corey and Ms. Jody are there."

So, on a Sunday afternoon, we hosted a birthday party for a beautiful little girl. There are so many stories that we could tell, but this one always reminds me that the house is doing exactly what the house was created to do. It's further evidence to me that the Isaiah 117 House is full of love, grace, goodness, and kindness on even the darkest of days. And I know that God is there. I know that His love is present because only God's love, grace, and light could take the place a child goes on their worst day and turn it into a place where they would want to have their birthday party.

Chapter Twelve

I feel like I am constantly saying some variation of: "If there is one thing I have learned through Isaiah 117 House, it's . . ."

Honestly, I finish the sentence differently every time. I tell people that this journey stretches us exactly how we need to be stretched. Isaiah 117 House is a faith journey that is molding and shaping and refining and bringing God's Word to life right in front of our very eyes. So, truthfully, by the time you are reading this, God will have revealed something new to me, and I'll be talking about it. But for now, I would like to finish that sentence in a few different ways, with a few of the lessons that God has been teaching me lately through this incredible story He's writing.

My hope, once again, is that through this book, you see God's heart more clearly. I hope that something I am learning resonates with you and stirs something inside your heart. That these simple lessons will serve as gentle reminders of God's goodness and His presence within our lives. And lastly, that through something you read, you begin to feel His invitation for you.

Lesson #1: God is near to the brokenhearted.

Prior to this foster care journey, I couldn't tell you what verse that is or what it really means, but now I've seen it. In the past few years, those words have come alive to me because I have seen God at work in the dark, messy parts of life. As I've said yes to coming alongside Him in the work He's invited me into, I've seen a lot of pain, but I've also seen a lot of God's glory.

It's a natural tendency, even for Christians, to try and avoid pain and brokenheartedness at all costs. And, who could blame us, right? Who wants to hurt? I see us do it for our children—

we do anything we can to minimize or avoid them ever having to experience pain.

But we have not been called to a life free of pain. We have been called to follow Jesus.

When you say yes to God, you will end up in messy, dark places because that is where Jesus is. He's calling us to bring light to those places, to step into the mess and to love people where they are.

For years I thought I had to earn God's love. Ironically, over the past few years I've worked my butt off, and through that process I've finally learned the truth. God doesn't love me anymore now than He did in 2013, 2012, or 2007. He just loves me. He created me and knit me together; He knows my strengths and my weaknesses, and He loves me. It's how He treats all His children.

Saying yes to Him doesn't make Him love us more; it simply opens our hearts for us to love God more. Want to hear something radical? Even if you're sensing God putting something on your heart to say yes to and you say no, *God loves you no less.*

However, if God is inviting you into something (and He always is) and you say yes, you will get to see a side of your God that you can discover no other way. You will see His mercy, kindness, and faithfulness, and you will know Him better.

I want to encourage you not to avoid pain. Don't step around the mess, but take hold of the Father's hand and step in—not only on behalf of those you will help, but also because, in doing so, you will see a side of your Savior that you would have never seen otherwise.

Lesson #2: "The Lord will fight for you; you need only to be still."

That verse, Exodus 14:14, became my verse years ago. I remember reading in Exodus one time about the parting of the Red Sea and recognizing something new. Right before the sea is parted, all God's people are standing around fussing, complaining, and screaming: "Where is God? Why would He bring us here? Moses, did you bring us here so that we could die?" Because when they looked around, they saw no way out. Red Sea on one side, hundreds of Egyptian soldiers on the other.

They were trapped, but then God showed up in a way they never saw coming. And right before He did—right before God gave Moses the miracle they needed—Moses shouted over the chaos, "The Lord will fight for you. You need only to be still."

There's so much power in the fact that Moses commanded the people to be still when there appeared to be no way out. Death was imminent. They felt forgotten; they felt ridiculous to ever have believed that there was hope in the first place. But God.

The people walked on dry ground through two towering walls of water to safety.

I now see so clearly how that verse helped prepare my heart for where I now stand. With so many of the children I meet, I feel stuck in the middle of chaos with no way out. There's so much pain, so much fear. And my temptation is to ask, where is God? Can He fix it? Is He coming? Does He care?

And then He shows up in a way that no one ever saw coming. He shows up, and children's lives are different because they see that, even on their worst days, they are not forgotten.

For the Israelites, it wasn't as if God made a way through the Red Sea and then life was fine and dandy. They experienced the miracle and then they wandered in the desert for forty years. For the children in foster care, few leave an Isaiah 117 House believing that their problems are all solved. But they absolutely see God move. They feel Him and know that He cares.

If God will perform miracles for children in our homes, He will also perform miracles for people outside our homes. And He will also perform miracles for people everywhere who feel forgotten and trapped and hopeless.

God is present. God cares. God will fight for us. We need only to be still.

Lesson #3: God is in the details.

I think when we're really sad, hurting, or mad, we can miss that. But even in the midst of the worst things, He is there. I hear stories all the time of people who have lost a spouse or a child, but in the details they see that God is still with them. That has definitely been the experience for Isaiah 117 House.

From seeing a white house with a red door in my head to seeing the first house that we bought that already had a white exterior and a red door —God is in the details. From choosing the name Isaiah 117 House to being invited to speak to the commissioner for foster care in Suite 117— God is in the details. And in getting texts like one I received recently from my program coordinator, that her general contractor handed her their Certificate of Occupancy at the exact moment her alarm went off at 1:17—God is in the details.

So often we try to pack a bag for a new arrival, praying and hoping that we choose things the child will like, and a little girl shows up and pulls out a pair of sparkly tennis shoes and exclaims, "These are the exact shoes I dreamed about!" God is in the details.

God is in the details and He cares about His children. And He is in the details of your life, too.

Lesson #4 There is freedom in obedience.

So often we feel like we can't say yes to God when He's inviting us in because it seems too big or too scary. We become paralyzed by the details and the how-tos and the what-ifs, and if we aren't careful, we waste a lot of time and energy swirling around in that fear and indecision.

But what I've discovered is that we don't have to have all of the answers before we say yes to God. God invites; we respond; God provides. There is so much freedom in that type of obedience.

Years ago I was a youth sponsor, and one of the slides we used for our worship lyrics was a picture of a silhouette of a man standing in the ocean. Both of his arms were stretched out into the air in a beautiful picture of praise and surrender as the sun was coming up. I made a big deal of that to the youth group. I told them I would do that the next time I went to the beach: stand in the water, put my hands up in the air, and have that same moment.

The next time I went to the beach, I thought about that picture every day. But I also kept thinking, *I'm gonna do it tomorrow, I'm gonna do it tomorrow*, until all of a sudden it was almost the last day. I thought, *Oh my gosh, I've made such a big deal out of this and the youth group will definitely ask me if I actually did it. I have to do it—at least so I can say I did.* So, on the last morning, I woke up early and went to the beach. It was so beautiful. Cool weather, gorgeous skies, literally nobody else around except one person over to the side. I made my way to the water and thought *Ok, hands in the air.* I went to put my hands up, and they stopped at my shoulders.

I couldn't make myself raise my arms. I thought to myself, *Oh my gosh, this is so silly. There's literally no one else even out here besides one person. Stick your hands up in the air.* I went to do it again, and again, my hands stopped. It was ridiculous. *What in the world is your deal, Ronda?* I told myself. *Stick your hands up in the air!*

I battled myself for a bit longer and then finally just threw my hands up. And all of a sudden, I felt peace. Once my hands were up and I was looking into the sky and being obedient in rest and surrender, I wasn't anxious. I didn't care who was looking, and I didn't care if I was doing it right. I didn't care about anything except praising the Lord.

We spend so much time with our hands in little fists by our shoulders, asking ourselves what happens if we don't do this right, or if someone is looking. We think our freedom and peace is found in staying safe and comfortable. But it's actually when we let go and surrender and throw our hands in the air that we find true freedom.

Jesus said that His yoke is easy and His burden is light, and it's true. Endless questioning and analyzing small details slow us down and make us feel heavy. But when we throw up our hands and say, "My answer is yes even though I have no idea what You want me to do," we actually enter into the freedom of obedience.

Then, even on the heaviest of days, we feel lighter. In the freedom of obedience, it's not about our own ability. We don't make things happen; we just walk in obedience. We don't move the mountains; we just believe that they can be moved.

Now, don't get me wrong here. There are days when it's dark and heavy and hard. It can't all be roses! But I've learned that, no matter what's going on circumstantially, there is a freedom in knowing that I am not in charge of anything, but simply walking in obedience.

God is bigger than me, bigger than Isaiah 117 House, bigger than all of it. And, He's bigger than whatever He is calling you to. Therefore, we can rest. Therefore, we can say yes to Him in freedom. My encouragement to you, friend, is to rest in that freedom.

Lesson #5: Love and grace are transformative.

I think we often lose sight of that and end up making it way bigger and more difficult. In the name of helping people change their lives, we set up complicated systems and programs and we plan out the perfect, magical thing to say to make a difference in someone's life. But nothing is more powerful than simple love and grace.

When children come to our homes, we don't have to have the right words for them. Children come into our homes, and they just sense it. They sense love and grace, and they react to it.

I got a message from a lady, who has now aged out of the foster care system, which said that because of the love she felt at the Isaiah 117 House she remembered that Jesus loves her, and it changed her. Nobody sat her down and told her that explicitly. We just got her a bath and showed her kindness. We got her clothes and fed her—no words involved. Just love, grace, and kindness. And it changed her.

I almost have to laugh at the simplicity of this lesson. 2,000 years ago, God sent Jesus to us because love and grace are transformative. That was the plan—to transform and make a difference through love and grace. The woman at the well ran back to her village to evangelize after meeting Jesus, and many came to Christ because of her. There was no system, no lecture that she sat through. She changed because she encountered love and grace. It doesn't have to be more complicated than that.

That's what an Isaiah 117 House is all about. We can't fix every problem. We can't change the whole system, but we can absolutely love children on their worst days. And it changes them.

Lesson #6: Do the next right thing.

A lot of people reach out to me wanting to open an Isaiah 117 House in their community, and we work with them to make that happen. It's a joy to see each new home that opens! But sometimes I talk to people who just want the blueprint of everything we did so they can copy it exactly.

I don't have a patent on any of this. This is God's project, not mine, and I'm grateful to share anything I know.

But what I hear from people in those instances is that their main focus is on wanting to make sure they don't mess anything up. They feel called to do something for God and want to arrive at the final product with as little resistance as possible. They want to have a step-by-step plan to be successful. And I get that desire.

But if I've learned anything through this process, I've learned that Isaiah 117 House has been a journey of faith. Our obstacles have not been with finances, workers, laws, or anything material—the primary thing that has threatened to hold us back is a lack of faith within our own hearts. Isaiah 117 House has been a journey of faith, and the best advice I can give to anyone asking is to just do the next right thing. The secret to the success of each Isaiah 117 House is that we just took it one day at a time, walking in obedience.

I have no idea what God is telling you about your next right step. I just know that if there is one "right" thing to do, it isn't to glue your eyes to a checklist, it's to fix your eyes on God.

God's invitation involves us learning to trust Him just as much as it involves our obedience. None of us is exempt from bringing His light to a dark world, but He's not asking us to know every answer along the way. He's just asking us to walk in faith and trust His provision.

One step at a time, one day at a time. Do the next right thing.

Lesson #7: Love, you are not alone.

When that line from Rachel Platten's song, "Stand by You," became the mantra for Isaiah 117 House, we couldn't have predicted how much it would resonate with people. We chose it for our original T-shirt design because that's our desire: for children, caseworkers, and foster families to know they are not alone.

But as the shirts began selling, and as people kept stopping me in airports and saying, "I have to know what your shirt means," I began to wonder what was so powerful about it. There seemed to be almost a kind of desperation from people to know more.

Then, it clicked. "Love, you're not alone" is the message of the gospel.

We are not created to be alone, and God has wanted His people to know they are not alone since the very beginning. He walked in the garden with Adam and Eve. He sent His Son to live among us. And when Jesus left, the Holy Spirit came to be in us and with us.

Because of the love of God, you don't have to do this life alone. God is with us.

That's why people are drawn in. Everybody can understand what it feels like to be alone, and everybody longs to know that they are not alone. And that's what God wants us to know— that we were never asked to do this alone. He is with us.

If that message of "Love, you're not alone" is for that child, and for that caseworker, and for that foster parent, then that same message is for me. And guess what? That same message is for you.

Love, you're not alone . . . He's inviting you in.

Chapter Thirteen

God truly is redeeming all things. Before Isaiah 117 House, I'd heard that phrase. I'd sung it. But I don't know that I truly understood it until one day when I was working on the first home. A little store in Piney Flats, Tennessee, was donating the countertops for the house, and when I went in to pick them out, a guy was there to help me. As I was getting ready to check out, he said, "Thank you so much for the work you're doing."

Up to that point, I hadn't been sure whether he knew why I was there or what the countertops were for. I responded, "Oh, you're so welcome."

This young man, probably in his late twenties, paused for a second longer, and then he said, "I can still smell the office from the day I was removed."

In my car, I reflected on what he had just shared with me. That little boy who had sat in a government office years ago and could still remember the smell had grown up, and he was now helping to install the countertops in a beautiful home for the next little boy. The beautiful redemption in that washed over me.

I've witnessed story after story like this. There was a gentleman who would show up to the Carter County House every morning at five o'clock to build the stairs. He had a story of being in foster care and going to prison and finding Jesus, and he literally felt like Jesus had asked him to come build us the steps in that old house. He came and worked every day for free. Anytime we tried to thank him, he'd tell us, "It's the least I can do for what Jesus has done for me."

There was a group of girls living in a place called Holston Home. It was a Christian group home, and sometimes girls would come to us before being placed there. Before we existed, the girls would have to sit in an office to wait. So they held a fundraiser. They made homemade salsa there at the group home, and they sold it to raise money for the Isaiah 117 House in Greene County because they wanted the next girls not to ever have to wait in an office like they did.

So much redemption has come through this ministry. I've even witnessed unexpected redemption in my own life. As I think about it now, I wonder how I didn't see it sooner, but also, it makes sense. It was 2017, and I was working hard trying to get the first home open. Isaiah was an eighteen-month-old, and Eli was a newborn. I was working a full-time job as a cheer and dance coach. I was also raising a thirteen- and ten-year-old. Life was crazy.

Corey and I were also part of a small group Bible study at that time. As part of the study, each of us was tasked with writing out our life story to share with the group. We did that by listing "fence posts"—major life events, good or bad, that had shaped us. We'd split into men and women, and each week a different person would share. I heard over and over the power of

God moving and working in these women's lives.

I didn't think much about mine until a few hours before I was supposed to share. I sat down that afternoon to jot down some life events, and one of the first things I had to write down was that when I was eleven, I was sexually assaulted by a teenage boy in my neighborhood.

And I had never told anybody. Well, I told a couple of girls at the time who were around my age, but I didn't tell my parents or any other adult for years and years. Decades. I spent my childhood trying to process what happened as best I could, but I remember so many times feeling so alone, so guilty, and so ashamed. So many times, I just longed for someone to say to me, "You know what? This is not your fault. You've done nothing wrong." But of course, I didn't give anyone the opportunity.

I kept writing down life events, and then I arrived at a more recent fence post. When I was forty, I started seeing a therapist, and I told another adult about what happened to me as a child for the first time.

I'll never forget her response. She looked at me and said, "Ronda, Satan did something very ugly to an eleven-year-old little girl. But God had very different plans for that little girl, and you are still here." It was the response I'd been needing for the last twenty-nine years. Her homework for me that day was to go home and picture an eleven-year-old little girl in my mind, and to write her a letter.

So I did. And that letter was full of the things I'd needed when I was younger. "Little one, you don't have to feel ashamed. You are not in trouble. You did nothing to deserve this. You are loved."

I had written that letter about two years before. And it wasn't until I began to write down another fence post—that I'm trying to start Isaiah 117 House for children who feel forgotten and guilty and alone—that my breath was taken away. It suddenly dawned on me. God, unbeknownst to me, was taking that ugly, nasty thing that happened to me at age eleven and was using it to make something beautiful. That little girl who so often felt ashamed and scared, who felt like she was in trouble and wondered if she had done something wrong to deserve what happened to her, was now providing a home for other children who know their own versions of those same feelings.

The little girl who needed an adult to see her and say that she was loved and not at fault had become an adult who could say those things to the next little ones.

God is redeeming all things. He took the ugliness of what happened to that little eleven-year-old and is using it to build 49 homes and counting across 10 states. I didn't know it and couldn't have planned it, but God had been working all along. When we're in the midst of the pain and the hard and the ugly, we can't see it; we just have to hold to what we know is true —that God is trustworthy, that He is powerful, that He redeems.

I hope this book is that reminder for someone. I hope that if you are in that place where you have yet to see beauty come from the ashes, this book will help give you the strength to hang on. His redemption is coming. God is redeeming all things. And now I know to my very core what that means.

Ronda Paulson is a native of Northeast Tennessee, a place she considers one of the most beautiful places in the world. She is married to her college sweetheart, Corey. They have four amazing children: Sophie, Mac, Isaiah, and Eli. They adopted two of them, but they can't remember which two! She would love to be a piece of leather on a beach somewhere, but instead she spends her days attempting to change the way foster care begins for as many children as possible!

facebook.com/isaiah117houseministries

Made in United States
Troutdale, OR
08/30/2023

12455045R00130